MANIFEST YOUR DREAMS

Find The Light In Your Storm and Ignite Your Purpose

By Christy Rutherford

Featuring – Debra Banks, Keshelle Davis, Emily Letran Shannon McGinnis, Debby M. Johnson, Holly Nunan

Manifest Your Dreams

Copyright © 2017 by: Christy Rutherford

ISBN-13: 978-1544167459
ISBN-10: 1544167458

First Edition for Print February 2017

Thank You

God, for using me as a vessel to impact the world

My family, for loving me unconditionally

Debby, Debra, Emily, Keshelle, Holly and Shannon, for believing in my vision and openly sharing your insight and gifts with others

Table of Contents

Preface

What's stopping you from going after your dreams and living the life you truly desire? Is it your past? Fear of failure? Fear of success? Time? Money? Don't have support from family and friends?

What are the reasons that you give yourself for staying where you are and then settling for a half-lived life rather than going for it? A lot of people feel that when they reach a certain income and position in their careers that they will be satisfied. However, according to a Gallup study, 80 percent of people who make over $100,000 a year drink alcohol compared to 45 percent of those who make less than $30,000. It's not the money.

Many people think that when they retire, they will have the security of a pension and will finally be able to do what they've always wanted to do. However, the job market today isn't as stable as it used to be, so is that the real reason? Also, people are checking out of here faster than the express checkout at a 4-star hotel. To think that you have the next 20 years or even tomorrow to go after your dreams is naïve. We aren't guaranteed tomorrow.

Many people think they don't have time to pursue their passions. Everyone is given 24 hours in a day. Your life and the results you have is solely determined by how you use your 24 hours. The people who are living their dreams and doing the impossible, invested their 24 hours into activities that got them closer to their destiny.

You don't have to give up your job to go after your dreams, but you may have to give up watching tv, football, basketball, reality shows and whatever else is on. You may have to give up the time you spend on social media.

If you frequent happy hours to drown out the disdain for your job, are you willing to invest that time into something that may work you out of your job? Are you spending hours on the phone complaining about your life, rather than reading a book or taking action to change it?

If you received $1440 every single day for 5 years and had to spend it within 24 hours or lose it, what would you do with the money? Would you blow it or would you get smart about investing it, so when the money stopped, you would be able to live out your dreams for the remainder of your life? We get 1440 minutes every day. Are you investing your time into activities that will get you to your dreams or are you blowing it?

Many people don't try because they feel their family and friends should fully support them. The vision that you have in your heart was given to you. No one else can see it. The dream is so big that it may seem like lunacy to everyone else but you. However, if you could do it by yourself, it's not a vision from God.

You will have to grow into the person that will fulfill the vision. There may be immense opposition and criticism from the people who are closest to you, but if you can't handle their criticism, then you won't be able to handle the criticism from others when you're highly successful.

With every blessing, there is a burden. Although TD Jakes, Joel Osteen, Oprah, Lebron James, Madonna, Beyoncé, etc., have impacted millions of people around the world by sharing their gifts, they are also harshly criticized. If you can't manage your "friend" talking about you, how will you handle the masses? If you want a higher blessing, you have to be able to manage a bigger burden.

Many people think they don't have enough money, but aren't willing to make any tradeoffs to pursue their dreams. If you have a nice house, nice car (less than 4 years old), can afford concert tickets, cable, a full cell phone plan, new clothes, get your hair and nails done regularly, then are you willing to adjust your lifestyle to achieve your dreams.

If you've maxed out the ways in which you spend your income, what are you willing to give up to free up some money? Moving into a smaller house or apartment? Driving an older model car or selling your car and taking public transportation?

Turning off your cable? Getting a pre-paid phone plan? Wear the clothes you already have and do your own hair and nails?

If these things seem appalling to you, are you really willing to give up a good life for a great life? The opposite of a great life is not a bad life. It's a good life.

Lastly, most people have stopped dreaming. They don't know what they want their life to look like and are so stuck in what their present circumstances are, they can't envision a new reality. They haven't gotten specific on how they want to live and feel, so the universe can't deliver what they desire. Is this you?

Most people know exactly how they want their coffee or lunch, but haven't thought about how they want to live in specific details. After finding your favorite combination, the coffee order rolls right off your tongue, "I want a grande toffee nut latte, soy, no foam, extra whip."

With predictability and expecting consistency, you know exactly what gets your taste buds going, "I want a grilled chicken sandwich with a side salad instead of fries, creamy Italian, croutons, sunflower seeds and a medium sweet tea with a little lemonade in it."

You know exactly how to order what you desire to eat or drink, but haven't put that same desire or specificity into your dreams. Hmmm……

Are you willing to look within yourself, get clear on what you desire and take the necessary action to make those desires a reality? Do you fear taking the risk and looking like a failure? Living your dreams is risky, but so is driving to work each day.

One question to really consider, "When you get to the end of your life, will you celebrate the life you lived or mourn the one you didn't?"

Successful But Unfulfilled?

What does success mean to you? Dr. Myles Munroe offered tremendous insight into the meaning of success. He said, "Success is the completion and the successful fulfillment of the purpose of your existence… Success is not making a lot of money. Success is not having a big house with a car by a lake. Success is not having a lot of friends and a lot of accolades and a lot of plaques on the wall. Success is really very very simple. It's you discovering your purpose and then completing it before you die... The only person who knows how successful you are is you and God."

Around the world, there are people who go to jobs every day that they hate. It doesn't mean they aren't well compensated for what they do or not offered security, but what they're doing may not be in alignment with why they are here.

I can remember points in my career where I would feel that I should be doing something different. I would say to myself, "The business world is missing me." Having several degrees in business, I would look out of the window from my office and almost feel a breeze on my face and then think about what my life would be had I chosen a different path.

Despite the challenges, I loved my job, the people I worked with and those that worked for me. I loved, loved, loved what I did, was paid well and was highly successful, but that didn't stop me from feeling like I wasn't in the right place.

We are all here to fulfill a purpose and for most people, our jobs are not our purpose. This doesn't mean that you're meant to be an entrepreneur, but it does mean that you are meant to serve others in some type of capacity. Happiness and fulfillment come through serving others.

After achieving high levels of success, some people want more. But more what? They feel that they should be doing more. But more what? They feel a pull, an energy that is guiding and directing them to do something. But do what?

It's shifting out of **success** and into **significance**. Making a true impact in the world and discovering your gifts and talents and using them to serve others. Significance will get you out of the bed in the morning, with your soul exposed and ready to set the world on fire with your passion for serving others. Significance is not about money, but money is usually a byproduct of significance.

Getting on the path to destiny is a ***decision***. It's a decision to surrender who you think you are and what you think you should be doing and start a journey into discovering who you really are and what impacts you are meant to make in this lifetime.

Looking at this image, you are born to carry out a plan - The Plan. However, you may have gotten deterred from The Plan once you graduate from high school and college, and took a job that wasn't in alignment with why you are here. You created a different plan - Your Plan.

As time has progressed, you may feel a pull and as I stated earlier, the call is for you to get back on the path of The Plan. It will be scary and you can feel like you are standing on a cliff and have to jump because you aren't in alignment with where you're meant to be.

If you make the decision to answer the call, then with time, surrendering and preparation, you have the opportunity to get into alignment with your destiny and far exceed anything you accomplished in your profession.

Success may or may not be measured in terms of money, but in the areas of joy, happiness, wholeness, serenity, health and peace. They will far exceed anything money can buy.

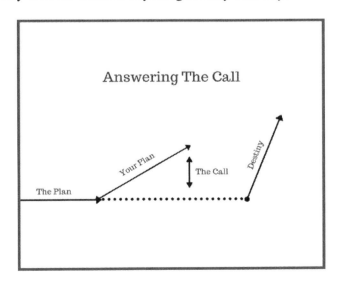

Your destiny will be connected to how you can to use your experiences and triumphs to serve others. Your greatest pain and the thing that nearly killed you will play a key role in discovering who you are meant to serve. If you felt immense pain, survived and learned the lessons from that perceived disaster or failure, then you're able to assist others with their pain. You have more compassion and empathy because you know exactly what they're going though. You can't put a price tag on real experience.

The 2017 Revelation

Leaders are INVINCIBLE, but I've learned that we are human too. One of my greatest challenges in life was burning out nearly five years ago. I've shared that story and plenty of others in the four books I published in 2016. In *Shackled To Success*, I shared that the story of my resignation may change based on how my perspective would evolve with time.

Was the story really true or was the truth based on how I perceived it at the time? If you are willing to grow, develop and evolve, you will see how each painful experience is used as a part of your purpose to serve others.

While attending Harvard Business School in January 2017, I had a revelation! Reading case studies and studying how large companies managed change, whether it was USA Today shifting from print only and then going online; when publishing companies had to shift from print to Ebooks; or when companies merged and two cultures had to become one. When there is disruption or when companies change, there are immense challenges that leaders are responsible for resolving.

After seeing myself reflected in the leaders of these companies who managed change and how hard it was to keep the culture of the organization intact, I thought, "Wait a minute!! Companies actually hire people to assist them with change?"

I didn't get that at any point of my career and had to learn the hard way, through the school of hard knocks. It wasn't just a cray cray boss that added to my burnout. It was managing constant change from the top of the organization while changing the local office.

As a leader and change agent, I was highly successful in protecting my personnel and getting incredible results in the whirlwind of change. I ensured that everything and everyone was taken care of but me, and that came at a high cost.

Back to the revelation… I realized the last two years of my career that I felt were detrimental to my health is one of my greatest gifts. I know what it's like to be in the fire of change and trying to manage the expectations of my leaders and create a culture of respect, loyalty and high performance for my personnel. I know what it's like to go home with headaches and with smoke coming from my head while working long and extended hours to drive results.

Leaders who are working to change their organization or create a culture of high performance have their work cut out for them. Doing it alone, without a blueprint or assistance can wreak havoc on them. Been there, done that.

This is a part of my purpose that has been revealed and I've recently expanded my business to reflect it. To share the framework of cultural change and lessons learned on the good and the bad, to ensure other leaders don't have the same fate.

The circumstances of what happened didn't change. My old boss was still a lunatic. The only thing that changed is how I chose to find more gems and lessons in my previous experiences and how I'll now use what I learned to serve the world. Do you see how this works?

Share Your Fruit

This book and my previous books are intended to serve as self-help books for leaders who feel overwhelmed and stuck in their circumstances. I feel that being a leader is the greatest gift that a person can offer mankind, but it is TOUGH!

Dr. Myles Munroe said, "A tree never eats its own fruit." My apple seed (dream) was planted, and I nurtured and grew my dream into a tree by eating (studying) the apples (fruit) of other world leaders. With growth, development, time and plenty of tough decisions, my dream became an apple tree and my books are the apples that I offer you.

Now it's up to you to eat the apples (study) to nurture your dreams and become an apple tree in an effort to offer your fruit to others. It's a perpetual cycle of service.

For this book, I wanted to share the stories of six phenomenal leaders, representing four countries and how they used their greatest pain and experiences to impact others. They are also apple trees who are sharing their fruits and I'm so grateful to be able to share their wisdom and insight with you.

This book is a compilation of interviews I did during two webinars in 2016. "Find Light In the Midst of Your Storm" and "Manifest Your Dreams and Ignite Your Purpose."

The ladies featured in this book are AMAZING and will give you plenty of insight to get you on the path to achieving your dreams. I've also included YouTube links to the original interviews, so you can listen as well. We had a great time!

I can't wait for you to read or listen to this book and get on your road to destiny. Your gifts are waiting for you to dig them up and bring them to the world. What are you waiting for?

Thank you for sharing this journey of discovery with me. It's been an honor and a blessing.

Chapter 1

Surrender Your Plan For THE Plan with Holly Nunan

Video – www.bit.ly/manifestdreams-Holly

Holly Nunan is an entrepreneur, mentor, speaker, blogger and children's book author from Australia. Holly was the owner of 65 franchises in the health and fitness industry and achieved her lifelong goal of retiring at the age of 31. Then she was able to pursue her purpose work. Holly built a global team in a network marketing company and generated over $1 million of sales yearly. She recently wrote and published her first children's book which became an Amazon bestseller, all within 31 days. She also hosts Powerful Parenting workshops that assist parents with expanding their children's consciousness, build their self-esteem and not place barriers on their limitless dreams and goals.

Holly, besides what we just read about you in your bio, tell us more about yourself.

Holly – I'm a mom of three little girls aged eight and under and I would be what I call a sort of Unbecome Activist. I'm an avid activist of assisting and guiding people in the unbecoming process, where they unbecome everything they're not…that they've been taught to be.

Christy – One of the things that's interesting about unbecoming is it takes a certain level of consciousness to understand because when I hear unbecoming, I think of pain because I've done that. But with the pain comes joy. It's letting go of who you thought you were and allowing God to do what He wants to do in you, so you can Become who you were meant to be to serve the children of the world.

When I think of unbecoming, it takes trauma and it takes pain to get to that state. You say it so eloquently, and as a teacher, it means you've had to have some pain in your life. So tell us the story or the most recent traumatic experience that you had that cracked open your shell to lead you on this path you're on today.

Holly – For me, it was just under two years ago. My husband got an incredible opportunity in business. The price we had to pay as a family in order for him to take the opportunity, was he had to go to Mexico and live for nine weeks. At that point I thought, "Yeah I can handle that."

We understand that success demands that you pay a price. We've kind of always done that, but once he left, oh my gosh it shook my world. I was basically a single mom of three little girls, who at the time were two, four and six. I had my dad who was living with me and he's an above knee amputee and had an operation on his other leg, so he was essentially crippled and feeling depressed about it. I had him living with us and three little girls struggling without their dad and wondering why their dad had been taken out of their world all of a sudden.

I had never done life without him before and it wasn't until then that I realized how much I was relying on other people, other sources to be my rock and other people to be my stability. What I realized was I was standing on quicksand, because when they left my life, even temporarily, I didn't know what to do with myself.

For me, the greatest pressure was having to continue being a blessing to other people, as I was leading a country in business and there were thousands of people counting on me to be the leader I had always been to help them grow and all these things. Having to bless other people while going through my own storm was incredibly challenging for me. My emotional rocket was so full and behind closed doors, life was so uncertain and I struggled in a very big way.

Christy – If you're missing a spouse, that causes pain. If you're caring for an elderly parent, that causes pain. You had three children under the age of six.

Holly – Yeah, and it was a grieving process. They were grieving. You know, my middle child wouldn't even talk to her dad when he called. I can't even explain the pain in her face if she was to see him on Skype. How do you tell a six-year-old why they can't see their dad? They just don't understand.

There were just mornings they would sit in the car and cry and wouldn't get out of the car and go to school. I took that on like, "I'm responsible for their pain."

I understand there is a logic behind pain and I do believe there is a purpose in pain and that pain is the point from which we expand. It's what shakes us up enough to wake us up, so that we can go through to the next level of consciousness and learn more about ourselves, but when you're in it, you can't see the wood from the trees sometimes.

Christy – One quote I love from Paulo Coelho, he said, "Difficulty is the name of an ancient tool created purely to help us define who we are."

What are some of the things that you did to take care of yourself, because once you realized you were relying on other people, what was that realization like and tell us what you did to come out of relying on other people?

Holly – I'm going to be really honest about this. My first response was I became a victim of my circumstances and I went into that little hole of, "I hate it being like this."

I wanted everything to change without taking responsibility for changing myself. I wanted someone else to solve the pain for me and make it better, and I had a moment where I just… Where… Really what it was Christy was I just made a decision to participate in my own rescue.

It's a principle that I definitely teach to a lot of other people and I went well, it's one thing to speak of this, but now here's my chance to be the example of everything I like to teach.

So, I started reaching out. I thought, "Okay what do I do from here? What's my next step?"

I reached out to my mentors, people that gave me wisdom and I opened myself up to them. I didn't try to be the strong Holly that I always saw. I allowed myself to be vulnerable. I learned how to swallow my pride. That was a big thing.

I think that was a lesson and a silver lining in the cloud for me. Definitely learning how to swallow my pride and ask for help, because up to that point, I was the person who was almost offended if you offered me help. I would interpret that as, "I can do it myself."

It was very hard for me to ask for help and admit that I was drowning. There were a lot of pride issues that I had to deal with and I realized through that, there is so much power in vulnerability. I'm sitting there thinking how can I go and lead these hundreds of people twice a week, and stand on a stage and lead them? How do I teach them congruently when my world is being shaken right now?

All those things were mental battles I had to fight and I started asking myself questions and that was really the beginning. I started going, "Okay, it is what it is. Ideal or not, it is what it is."

More importantly than just asking the question, the most important part was, I started to think of a solution to the answers. I didn't ask questions just for the sake of being a victim and going why why why? It was like, no really, why?

Why is this and what am I supposed to get out of this? If I don't learn the lesson, it's going to keep repeating, and I don't want this to keep repeating. That was it for me. I started participating in my own rescue, reaching out to people and humbling myself enough to say, "I'm struggling. Can someone help me?"

Also, actively putting myself in the environment that would feed my spirit and purposely getting in touch with people that gave life to me, instead of just sitting in my little hole feeling sorry for myself.

Christy – Holly you said so much in that and I'm going to try to wrap it all together. One of the challenges that leaders have, I think it's women, but men do it too, but especially women, we make sure that everyone around us is taken care of. We make sure everyone around us is fed and we give, give, give, give and we don't take care of ourselves.

I equate it to having an oxygen tank, where you have 20 people standing around you and they're looking at you. They have an oxygen mask attached to your tank and they have their own oxygen mask. They have both of them, and you don't have anything.

You're laying on the ground without oxygen and they're looking at you, holding the oxygen mask attached to your tank. They're sucking the life out of you and they won't offer your oxygen back.

You learn who's sucking the blood out of you, or sucking the life out of you. What do you have to say about checking your circle? You also talked about being around mentors and people that you could listen to and being vulnerable. They're not the same set of people.

Talk to us about the people who will suck the life out of you and what you had to do to distance yourself from them in an effort to allow yourself to be able to be fed by other people.

Holly – I distinctly remember the process. It was this moment where... Exactly what you said, you've got to be aware of, you've got to be so conscious of your associations and your environment and where you're putting yourself.

For me there was this moment where I got off a call with one of my mentors, who gave me a little bit of tough love, which is exactly what I needed at that time. First of all, I cried. I've always been this hard core, tough, I can handle anything kind of person and I cried, and you know what, I allowed myself to feel it.

Number one, I believe that you can't heal what you can't feel. So I gave myself permission to just let myself feel it and let myself be in it and to believe that there was purpose in the pain. I kind of started to realize at that point that pain teaches you lessons that your pride won't allow you to learn because I had already started to see some lessons in all of that.

I definitely distanced myself from people. I was just so conscious, do you give life to me, or do I feel like you take life from me? I loved myself enough to give myself permission to be selfish. Not selfish with the intentions of hurting other people. That was not my intention.

My intentions were, "I'm going to give myself permission. I'm going to love myself enough to take care of me. Being aware of that, I understand that there are casualties in every war and even though my intentions are not to hurt other people, I'm aware that my decisions might hurt them, and I needed to be okay with that."

That doesn't make me a bad person because my intentions are **not to hurt you**. My intentions are to **take care of me** and if the byproduct of that is going to hurt you, well, I need to give myself permission to be okay with that.

Because here I am right now, I'm supposed to be the hero. I'm supposed to be the leader. I'm supposed to be the one that can throw everyone a rope, but you can't throw anyone a rope when you're in the water drowning with them. You've got to get yourself back in the boat first before you can throw anyone a rope.

The price that I had to pay to get myself back in the boat was to basically not consider anyone else's feelings. To be okay with saying I don't have space for you. I don't have space for what the effects of my decision might have on you. I've got to take care of me and my intentions are not to hurt you, but if you become a casualty in this war, then I'm okay with that.

Christy – Wooooo weeee!! That's good!! It's so true that people are hurting and drowning. You're a powerful woman. I've met you and I see a lot of myself in you and it's funny that we have a lot of the same challenges, but we also resolved our challenges in the same way, which is The Way.

It's almost like we'll drown and we'll be in pain and we won't cut other people off because, in some ways, we created the situation, so there's guilt around it. You talked about it, but the day you make the decision that you're going to cut people off or you're going to die. Either you're going to change or you're going to die and when you get that point, and it's a very very painful point to get to, then you become distant and people call you selfish and people call you names, but you feel better.

There's a better feeling when you cut people off. I urge people to know that it's okay to let people go, even if you created their dependency on you, because they will suck you dry and they don't know that they're doing it, but you have to care about yourself enough to separate yourself from them.

Holly – This is something that made me feel better about the fact that I had to do that. I went, okay, I know that people come into my life to give me lessons and I'm in their life to give them lessons, and I feel that there's some kind of peace around the fact that I need to let you go, and that peace that you feel is God.

It's your internal guidance system saying, "This is what I need you to do in order to be the lesson that person needs."

I understand that I may have caused you some pain and I can feel guilty over that. I will feel guilty if I don't give you that pain because if making this decision feels right to me, then not making it, is essentially taking a lesson from you, because the universe is trying to use me to give you one of your lessons.

I don't just get messages, I'm also the messenger. So if I take away that pain or if I don't make a decision because I'm trying to help you avoid your pain, then essentially, I'm not contributing to your expansion.

If I really do care about you, I'll make the decision that I need to make and you'll get your lesson from that. If it means that I'm one of your lessons, then it's wrong of me to interfere with the bigger plan and not be that lesson.

Christy – Woooo! SMOKIN!!! So much truth!!!

What are two things that you did to change the trajectory of your life from that pain point, because it's not something that's going to occur overnight and it's typically a process, but it starts somewhere. What are two things that you can share that helped you shift from that low point in your life to get you out of the hole that you were in?

Holly – Number one, be aware of what you're saying when you talk to yourself. I really started to commit to myself that I can handle anything. I believe that everything will be alright in the end, so if it's not alright, it's not the end. This is just the process.

The two things that I would sum it up with is, number one, just embrace the pain. Don't hate the pain. Don't resist the pain, because resistance just brings more energy into what you're attracting, so you've got to practice the art of allowing and you do that by practicing pain.

Number one, embrace the pain, let yourself feel it. It's not wrong, find peace in the pain. Number two, practice faith. Feeling the pain, I may not like it because I understand and I do have enough knowledge to know that nothing happens by accident. Everything is always on purpose and if I look back at points in my life where I've become a better person, I already have the evidence that proves to me that all of those times came from pain points in my life.

This is just another point and I've got to see myself beyond this moment. Life is a whole lot bigger than just this one moment. That allows you to embrace it and once you've essentially become comfortable with feeling uncomfortable, then you practice faith.

What I mean is, you believe in what you can't see. You don't need to know how you'll get out of it, you just need to know you will. You don't need to know exactly what the next step is, you just need to know there is a next step, and you need to be ready for it. Love yourself enough to let go.

Christy –When I think about where I was four years ago and I'm doing this interview of "Find Light In the Midst Of Your Storm," as an ode to that time period because I was in a storm that lasted so long, I didn't know what was going to happen.

I didn't know how, but I was watching Oprah videos. I was overweight. I had arthritis. I was miserable and drinking wine all the time, but I had all this money and success. So on the surface, I was successful, but at home, when I was alone, the pain came.

I remember Maya Angelou saying, "On the other side of every storm is a greater sense of joy."

My life changed when I started to practice faith and I started to see myself out of that situation and that's when your words become congruent with your action of faith and you say to yourself, "I don't know what's going to happen, but I know it's going to be okay."

Share with us how to practice faith and how you got to that level to have peace with the pain. It starts with that trajectory of I'm going somewhere. I have a vision of who I'm going to be. I just know that I have to go through pain to get there.

Holly – I use a lot of pictures in my mind. How I force myself to see myself beyond it is to see myself in hindsight. I love being on stage. I love teaching and leading and I would see myself telling this story.

I could see how I would use this story, not while I'm in it, but once I'm done with it, and instantly I was able to see how many people I would be able to reach because of this story. How many lives I would be able to touch. How many people would open themselves up even further to me and the messages I had because of this story.

It kind of humbled me and gave me an extra ability to relate to people. You can only impact those that you can relate to.

When people can't relate to you, when people don't see themselves like you, basically, you lose your credibility. Your advice sounds loopy, you don't know what it's like to be me, you can't help people.

I would say, "I know I'm in this now, these times don't come to stay, they come to pass."

It's what Les Brown said, "These times have come to pass."

When these times pass, how will I use it? That's how I was able to give myself evidence in my mind that I'm on the other side of it because I can see myself talking about it on a stage. I can see myself on an interview like this being able to share it with people, who are now sitting on the other side going through it, so it is going to be okay.

Someone can say to themselves, "I can't see that it's going to be okay, but it was okay for her and now I have enough evidence to just feel safe with where I'm at."

That's how I did it. I would see this situation in hindsight and that was all I personally needed to go, "It's okay. I've seen the other side and I just need to embrace this while I'm here and learn about myself."

How I learn about myself? I let myself feel it. All my life, I blocked everything. I just had this high wall around my heart and I would deal with emotional situations like, "Why am I going to let that hurt me?"

If I'm tougher, then nothing can hurt me and it stopped my ability. It put walls between me and people I wanted to help. I wasn't able to have an open heart. I didn't have space to take on anyone else's feelings or emotions because I was too full of my own stuff.

That's why I say it was the hardest point of my life and the best point, because it was where I learned to let myself feel it. Once I was able to let myself feel it, I was able to heal it. I was able to get a lesson out of it. I was able to see what it was trying to teach me. I was not only able to ask questions, but I was able to sit there and let myself hear the answer.

Christy – You answered this perfectly. It's about focusing on where you're going to be, as opposed to where you are, and knowing that, holding on to that, and believing that.

Holly – That's what faith is. You don't need faith when you understand something. When you understand something, you don't need faith, you use knowledge. You need faith when you can't understand. The only chance you get to practice faith is when you don't understand. When you can't see a reason right now, but you believe there is one. That's what faith is.

You don't go, "Well, I just can't understand why this is happening, so I can't use my faith because I don't understand."

That's the whole point, you're not supposed to understand, because if you understand it, you don't need faith. Faith is something you use when you can't understand. You just trust in something else that is a whole lot more powerful than you.

Christy – Napoleon Hill talks about "applied faith" and I didn't understand what it meant until I *became it*. Applied faith is more than just studying the Bible. It's about *becoming the scriptures* and really believing that faith is belief in the things unseen.

TD Jakes calls it "Revelation in Retrospect." He said, "For every problem in your life, there's a purpose that you don't see. You're looking at what happened and God is looking at why it happened, and you'll never be able to praise him about the *what* until you look at the *why*."

That's exactly what you said. He also said, "Purpose isn't always visible. Problems are visible, but purpose is not visible, it's invisible."

So you are here to serve someone for a reason. Your life isn't necessarily for you and you're not being selfish for you. It's when you surrender to grow and become that person to serve other people, then you feel better, and you love life more and you feel more.

Tell us more about the surrendering process and what advice do you have for our readers who are having challenges and they don't know if they can hold on. What advice do you have for them?

Holly – Let me say this, the letting go process. Here's what I'm passionate about teaching. Why is it so hard to let go? Why are we feeling this pain and what are we supposed to let go of? I've been told that I need to let go of my resistance, but what exactly am I supposed to let go of? What is it that I'm holding on to in the first place? I didn't realize I was holding on to something. I don't even want to be like this.

Here's what it is. There's a payoff that you're getting for being like that. I guarantee it! Anytime you're stuck in a place of pain, it's because you won't let go of something. Whether it's that part of you, that identity that you've attached yourself to that doesn't belong to the next level of you. To go to the next level of consciousness, you can't take anything from this level with you.

You have to basically die. You know, the pain is basically like a death process. You're supposed to be dying to who you are up until that moment, so you can become who you're meant to be after that moment. For me, it was really like being real with myself and asking, "Why won't I let that go?"

You know why, because there's a payoff you get for that. For example, it's the story of my husband being away. At the time, it's like, what is it about me that doesn't want to give up this pain? Because if I really don't want to feel it, why don't I just let go of it? Here's what it was…

At the moment, that's how I got access to other people's love, energy and care because every time they see me, what do they say? My story is, "Oh you know my husband is away. I'm on my own and dah dah dah." Now, that gets me attention from people.

That's how at that time, subconsciously, I was accessing recognition, love, care, feeling valued, feeling important, and feeling cared for by people. That was my story and if I was to give up that story, I'm not the poor lady with the three kids that's got a husband away at the moment.

If that's not my story anymore, then what will people care about? What reason would people have then to show me love or to show me care or to show me compassion? Because at the moment, I'm a victim of those circumstances and every time people see me, they ask, "How are you? How are you coping? Oh my gosh, it must be so hard without Greg."

And I felt like a tough little hero. "Oh my gosh, you're so amazing. You're doing so well."

Those were all of the payoffs I was getting. I'm attached to this story. That's how I'm accessing feeling significant, feeling like I'm somebody. You've got to work out what your payoff is and you've got to be willing to give that up. That's the hard part.

Christy – WOOOO WEEEE!!!!! Holly you're AMAZING!!!!! Thanks again for sharing your tremendous wisdom and insight with our readers. If this didn't shift them, I'm not sure what will. I love it, love it, love it!! Thanks so much!!

Surrender Your Plan For THE Plan

Chapter 2

Finding Light In My Shattered Life with Debby Montgomery Johnson
Video – www.bit.ly/manifestdreams-Debby

Debby Montgomery Johnson is the President of Benfotiamine.Net Inc, a vitamin supplement company that provides an alternative for the pain of neuropathy, a nerve disorder. She recently expanded her Purpose by releasing her book and starting her movement, *The Woman Behind The Smile*. Debby shares her story of betrayal that turned into a financial disaster and she removes the mask of shame and shows others how to do the same. She's now a speaker, trainer, and inspiration to many women that are ashamed of something, through no fault of their own, keeps them hiding from each other and the world.

Debby, besides what we just read about you in your bio, tell us more about yourself.

Debby – As I'm thinking about business and the things that I've done, right now I'm most grateful for being a daughter, a sister, a proud mother of four, mother in law of two and grandma of three and a new wife. The most important thing in my life right now is my family and that came about with what we are going to talk about today.

Christy – The reason why I wanted to do this series is because sometimes when we're caught in the darkness, we never think we're going to get out of it. Storms and tough times don't last always but tough people do.

Jim Rohn said, "The same wind blows on us all."

If we live long enough, we will see that life is like a roller coaster. Sometimes we have highs, sometimes we have lows. Tell us what happened with you and your life and how you got to where you are today with being grateful for everything you have.

Debby – Life started a long time ago. I'm in my mid-50's and was married for nearly 26 years. Six years ago I was at a business meeting. I was a treasurer for a local elementary school and was at a school board meeting. I had my phone off and during a break, I never check my phone during breaks, but that day I did. My phone was lit up. I had 12 messages waiting for me and I picked up one from my oldest son and when I listened to the message, it was very short, brief and to the point.

He said, "Mom, dad died. I'm coming home and I'm taking care of everything."

I listened to that call over and over and saw that the other calls were from my parents. They didn't get me because I had my phone off and that particular call from my son changed my life forever. That was the most incredible moment, because your life...it stops for a second and you have to regroup.

I'm not sure if that was the low, but that was the beginning...the catalyst to the next few years of an interesting life.

Christy – In that moment and in that dark spot, how long did that last for you? You said it wasn't the low, so it got lower. Share with the readers about the lower level than what just happened there.

Debby – From what happened there, I think at that point when you get something so traumatic given to you so quickly, totally unexpected. Lou was not sick. He was traveling and had left the day before. I said goodbye on a Wednesday and said, "See you tomorrow night when you get back home" and when that phone call came I realized that my life as I knew it was forever changed.

I wasn't going to have the plans that we made. They weren't going to be fulfilled. Every year we'd sit down and laugh that each year we'd plan at the first of January and whatever we planned never really happened. But now I knew it wasn't ever going to happen because he was gone.

I'm a really spiritual person so I realized that one day we'd be together on the other side, but for the immediate future I was 51 years old and had four children. Fortunately, the oldest three were either in college or the military and I had my 15-year-old here at home.

My life at that point was, I've got to get to Maddie, my youngest, before anyone else can talk to him. Which is a very strange thing, but in the light of social media, Facebook and Instagram and all these things that we and the kids use instantly, in spite of not having phones in school.

I knew that if I didn't get to Maddie right away, somebody else would. My mind went, "I have to get home. I have to get over to the school and I have to get Maddie away from school so that he hears it from me."

That's what happened. I had friends who gathered my stuff. They drove me home. When I got to my house, there were cars everywhere. I don't know how people found out so quickly. I sat there for just a moment and had girlfriends already planning how to get Lou's body back here. How to get my parents over to where he was. He passed away on the west coast of Florida, and we live on the east coast.

Once he left home on Wednesday, I never saw him again, which in itself is a whole 'nother story because there was no closure. My immediate to-do list at that point was to get over to the high school to pick up Maddie. He's actually written a story about that, as it was one of the most traumatic times in his life because I had never gone over and taken him out of school without notice before.

Actually that was one of the worst times ever because I couldn't control anything. Here was my 15-year-old son just falling apart. We had to come back home. From that point on, it was prepare, get all the phone calls made. Get my other three children back home, and get my brothers and their family.

It was something that you wished you prepared for in advance and I had some preparation, but who expected it? Especially at my age. I knew that Lou would never live forever. He was a really big guy. He had diabetes and some other health issues, but no heart problems and he died of a heart attack. It was no notice, quick and from that point on it was…get things in order, take care of the family, get them down here, and get the memorial service.

Here is the hardest part. That week, Lou and I were preparing to go up to Fort Rucker in Alabama, because my second son, Charlie, was an Army helicopter pilot and he was graduating from flight school and we were supposed to go to the flight school graduation. That didn't happen for me.

My oldest son Christopher, who's a Marine Corps pilot, came in and he, Maddie and Charlie took a brother's road trip the week I prepared for the funeral. It was a bonding experience for them, but was something that unfortunately I got left out of. That was the hard part for me. To see the kids dealing with it. Christopher was thrown into growing up in a second. In a phone call, Christopher was 23 years old and he instantly became the man of the house. It was an amazing experience.

That didn't really get you to my low point. My low point was probably six months later. The first six months you're just on autopilot. You're just in animated suspension. I was working two jobs, at the elementary school and then I was running the company that Lou had started and left me with suddenly.

After about six months, I probably realized, "Dang, I'm going to have to do all of this by myself now and really do it."

Then I realized in the middle of the night that I was there by myself for the first time in 26 years. I was sleeping by myself in a king sized bed and I think I used a foot and a half. That was the lonely part. For me, that was the loneliest part when I realized finally that I was going to be by myself, at least for that period of time and I needed to make something of the family and the company and myself.

Christy – That's interesting because one of the questions that I had for you was, you immediately got to work. You said you were on autopilot, so you didn't really get to internalize what happened. The internalization of your new reality, did that occur six months later or were you able to do it within that period?

Debby – I think little by little. I'm a very self-sufficient person, so I went into left brain mode. I realized what had to be done. I realized that the company he created, I didn't know anything about. I just packed packages at night, so I needed to learn how to keep his business going.

I was making $24,000 a year as a school treasurer. The only reason I worked there is because I got benefits. It wasn't going to pay my mortgage or the things that needed to be paid. My company was going to pay the bills and I needed to learn how to run the company. That's where the realization of "get your act together and use your resources" came in.

That's what I needed to do. Find out who the people were that knew the most about Lou running this company. It was our vendors, our best customers, and our wholesale customers. I ended up calling them and told them what happened and said, "I would really appreciate your help. How did Lou do this with you?"

They were incredible. Step by step, people walked me through how to order new product. How to find out where the customers were and how to even do the packages. What's the postage and all that kind of stuff. Step by step, people helped walk me through it and that kept the company going as best I could do.

As far as being prepared with the finances, that was the most incredible thing, because we had life insurance for 35 years. Between the two of us, we had life insurance forever and that year Lou turned 56 and his life insurance premium went from $100 a month to $500 a month and he refused to pay it.

Here I was with four children under the age of, whatever it was at that point, and I'm like, I can't afford not to have life insurance. "Lou what if something happened to you?"

He said, "Oh no problem. We've got investments down in Costa Rica."

He came up with all these excuses, that we had these investments and how we'd be taken care of in 5-10 years. So, he went and canceled his life insurance policy.

I let it go for another two months and he saw that I was still paying it. He was furious. He called them up and said, "I don't want this anymore!"

He ranted on and on and on and finally, they canceled the policy. Two months later, I got the phone call that he died and I'm sitting there with no life insurance.

I had no fallback and no extra pool of money to keep things going and that's the realization that I have to keep the company going because that's the only way I'm going to keep the family going. That was the only time that I really got mad at him. Of course, there was nothing he could do at that point, but I was angry that he was so shortsighted in canceling the life insurance policy because he'd just spent $500 on a stupid widget for his race car.

Anyway, that's water under the dam, but that was one time in my life that I got a little upset that I needed security and all those years, I'd finally gotten great security with his company and with everything. All of the sudden, I don't have a husband. I have a company I don't know how to run and I have no fallback. No insurance, no nothing.

That was a real slap in the face. I said, "Okay Deb, put your boots on and get yourself going!"

You asked me a question once about what I learned about myself. I learned that I could be self-sufficient. That I would take responsibility for myself and for the family and that I could just do it! I could just do whatever I wanted to. I just needed to think about what I needed to do and then get the guts to say just do it! Just do it. One day at a time. Sometimes one minute at a time. But I just did it.

Christy – That's the question that I was going to ask because I know you now and I know that you're pretty tough. Typically, with women who are tough and super spiritual, there's something in their past that creates that toughness in them. Mental toughness comes through challenges. It comes through standing up in the storm and standing up in the challenges and not shrinking back.

When you talked about being self-sufficient and responsible and just doing it and getting the guts one day at a time or one minute at a time, what actions did you take? What did you say to yourself to get yourself out of the bed in the morning?

Debby – I had to. For the six months after he died, I kept the two jobs. I had to get up in the morning to go to the elementary school and I adjusted my schedule so I was there from 7 in the morning until 1 or 1:30. Then I would do something for myself. I would go swimming every day.

Every afternoon, I would go to the YMCA and I would do laps. I would do lap upon lap upon lap. It was routine. I did five laps of this and five laps of the next stroke. It was very routine. I don't stray from what I do, so if I get in a routine, I do it.

The whole time I'd be going up and down the pool, I'd be talking to Lou. I'd be having these conversations with him, and I would say, "Am I doing the right things with the kids?"

If I got frustrated about something from the office, it was really silly, but I would say, "You got to show me. You got to give me the password. You got to help me learn how to do such and such."

I would keep my conversation going with him. Someone said it wasn't really with him, it was with my own self, which it was. But it was my way of being comforted that, okay, he's listening and he may not be able to tell me specifically, but he'll show me somehow. That gave me great comfort and it kept me on the right path.

I did that until I realized at one point during the summer that I was making more money with the company in one month than I made in the whole year working with the school. So why was I killing myself with two jobs?

I needed focus on the company and where it would take me from there. That's what I did. I gave up my school job. I gave up my medical insurance. That was a big leap of faith to understand that I could take care of myself. It was going to cost me a lot more money, but I needed to be able to focus on the business at hand and make it grow.

That's what I've had to do in the last six years is to take the company from what Lou did. It's because I wanted to honor his business. Honor his legacy by keeping the company going and that's what I've tried to do day by day. I strive to do it, I don't try to do it. I strive to do it day by day and to make him proud of what the business is all about.

Did I answer your question in a round about way?

Christy – You did. You know I love you Debby. One comment that you made stood out...about being comforted and talking to Lou and asking him to help you and knowing that he would show you. Your conversation was moving you forward. It wasn't a self-defeating conversation.

Do you credit that with how you dug yourself out of the hole, because you were still moving forward and you were asking for help, but you weren't focused on what didn't happen in that moment?

Share with the readers more about talking forward. Did you do that all the time or did you have those times where you fell backward? What did you do the most?

Debby – I've always felt that way. Things have happened in my life which have been sad in a lot of ways, but I've never portrayed myself as a victim. I've always been the one that says, "Learn from whatever just happened. This is an opportunity for growth and what can you learn from the bad that's happened?"

Lou lost his job a couple of times in our married history. It could have been some personal issues with losing children. All of us have the wind of life blow over us and I just realized that God only gives me something I can handle.

I may not know how to handle it, but there is always a friend or someone around that is my little angel. My personal angel that can help me move forward and I don't like to stand still. You can't stand still. You're either going backward or you're going forward and I knew I needed to go forward in whatever way I could.

The best way for me was I found other women business owners that could propel me towards what I really wanted to be. I wanted to find my passion in being an entrepreneur. My passion in being a woman. My passion in being a speaker. Whatever I wanted to do.

I needed to get away from my home. I run the company from the house on my computers. I have an internet company. I deal with people on the telephone, but I didn't deal with them in person. In addition to my lap swimming, I started going to a water aerobics class at 8 o'clock in the morning. Again, doing something for me because I realized after giving myself to everybody else that if I didn't fill myself up at some point, I wasn't going to have anything left to give anybody else.

I had to start physically. I had to get out and I loved being in my water aerobics class. I'm the youngest one by about 20 years. I want to be like the ladies that I'm swimming with. They're all like my mom, they're great. That's how I would start my day. Then, I could come home and be by myself running the company.

It was one minute at a time. Literally one minute at a time, but to surround myself with good, positive influences and not be around the naysayers. Especially when you're by yourself, people say you can't do that or that's not a good thing for you and you really start internalizing that you can't do stuff. I'm like, "I've always been able to do stuff."

I'm not going to let people who are negative stay around me. As I've gotten a little bit older, I've learned how to say no to some things and I've learned how to say I'm sorry to some things. I feel like I own myself now because there's one thing someone asked me when Lou died, it was a good friend of his and he said, "Okay. So you're 51 years old, now what are you going to do? Who are you going to be now? You've been a wife. You've been a mother. You've been a daughter. You've been all these things. Who are you, Debby Butz Montgomery?"

I said, "Dang! I don't know."

I need to figure out who I am and what I want to do. It's taken some time to do that. It took Lou dying to push me forward to really find out who I am because I am very accommodating to my children, my family and my husband. I did everything for everybody else as best I could and now I was thrown into a position where I needed to do something for me so I could keep this going on for everybody else.

Christy – Debby, you talked about surrounding yourself with good, positive people. When you're down and around people who will allow you to feel sorry for yourself, they speak fear into you and they coddle who you are until you don't want to be that anymore.

A lot of people don't know that when they want to change or they want to change their circumstance, they have to change the circle of the people that they're in because they will hold you hostage to being that person who's sad or depressed or not able to move forward or get over something.

What's your advice to our readers on minding the company they keep?

Debby – I tell this to my youngest son all the time. I say you have to change. If you're in a difficult situation and you want to move out, you have to change people, places, and things. You have to be ready and you have to be good to go and in the internal spectrum. You have to be ready to go.

You could die tomorrow. That's what I learned about Lou dying at such a young age. It could happen to any of us at any moment. When it's your time, it's your time and don't have any regrets. Don't hold grudges. If you have to ask for forgiveness of somebody, do so. Put your pride behind you.

I've had to do this with family members. I've had to say I'm sorry. I'd done something that they didn't like and I didn't know that I had done it, or for some reason, they saw that I didn't have respect for something that they did.

I always try to be a good person, but there are going to be times when we hurt other people's feelings or whatever. We need to be kind and humble and accept we're not perfect. We're taking steps to become perfect, but we're not perfect and we just have to be strong and powerful in our own ways. Move forward and be willing to put the negativity aside. Get away from it and do the best you can.

You can't change your past, but you can change your future. We're not our past, but we've learned from our past. Like I said, you have to keep moving forward. You can't just sit on the fence because then you're good for nothing. I tell people to be prepared for whatever it is you need to do to be the best person you could be. To be kind. To be humble. To be respectful. To be genuine.

To stand up. My new mantra for now is, "Stand Up In Your Own Power!"

Speak up. Don't let other people do things to you, let them do things with you and try to be as positive as possible. Put a smile on your face. Maddie was walking with someone this morning and I was teasing this friend of ours because he's a grouchy old man.

I said, "Merle, be as happy as I am!"

He said, "How are you so happy every day."

I said, "It's my choice."

I make the choice to smile in the morning. I make the choice to jump out of bed and go swimming or do whatever. I make the choice to do my hair or put on some makeup and feel good for me. Not for anybody else. Feel good for me and then when I'm standing in my own power and I'm being happy, then those around me can be happy.

That's a self-fulfilling prophecy. You be happy and people around you will be happy. So make someone's day by being kind. That's what I do.

Christy – I agree and that's one of the things that Eckhart Tolle talks about all the time. William George Jordan's book was written in the early 1900's and he talked about serenity and being calm. He said something like, the calm man can make everyone around him calm, but we can't expect calmness and joy if we're not giving it off to other people.

If we're secretly unhappy, that's the thing. It's not about smiling and painting on a smile in the morning, it's about, how do you really feel?

How do you really feel at night when you're alone by yourself because that's how you're going to show up in the world. It is possible to become as happy as you are because you choose it every single day and you choose to do things that make you happy.

You choose to smile and you choose to not allow people to take advantage of you. You choose to stand up in your own power and you choose to say no. Every day you can choose happiness or you can choose fear. You can choose joy or you can choose chaos.

What are two things you did that changed the trajectory of your life and how you feel about yourself today?

Debby – I realized that for all the years that I was married I don't like contention and I still don't like contention. I would stuff it at that point. I would not talk about it. If something was going wrong or something was happening that I didn't like, I didn't stand up and talk about it. Nowadays I do.

I actually got remarried. I've been married for six months to a wonderful guy, but from the very beginning, I said, "Look, I want to be different this time and I had great times in my marriage and I had lousy times in my marriage. Going forward, I want to be honest in my feelings with you and I want to be able to speak about it."

So if I ever have any issues or if he ever has any issues with me, we go for a walk. We hold hands and we talk. It is the best thing ever because there's nothing that we're holding back. It's all done in love and calm. We've not had a fight, knock on wood, but we've had good discussions.

That's what I've chosen to do, to be completely honest in my feelings, but reserve the right to be kind to others. You know, you can't be nasty when you're telling someone how you feel. Be kind and be honest forthright and don't let people step on you.

I'm not a doormat. I'm a strong woman. I'm accommodating, but I want to be able to do some good in the world and show women that they can stand up and speak for themselves in a very calm, quiet way, but in a very strong way.

I think that's what a lot of women, especially my age, have missed all these years. They're not really themselves any more.

They put up that mask of trying to look perfect and we're not. We all had something that happened in our past. We need to own it, be responsible for it, move forward from it and do something positive in the world.

Maybe I'm Polly Ann'ish today, but that's me. A lot of bad things happened, which is okay. I found that you have to forgive the past and move forward.

Christy – Forgiving the past is the only way you can move forward. It takes a lot as you go through tragic times, but as you come out into the light, you look back and see that the bad experience actually propelled you forward.

If you choose to get up, you can use it as a launch pad to your destiny or to your next level. If you fall down and you stay down and then self-medicate or just stay in the mess, without forgiveness, it will hold you hostage to something that you don't want anymore. That's what a lot of people miss.

Debby – That's true and I found the best way to get out of that is to do service to somebody else. Put yourself out there. I would be grateful that I had my own problems when I was out helping others because I'm looking around going, "I wouldn't want their problems."

My issues were something that I could manage and when you do service for somebody else your heart is with them and you're not internalizing everything about yourself. There's no pity party when you're out there helping somebody else.

That's the key, to get away from your own problems and help somebody else out and maybe you're going to help them out because of your problem and what you've been through. Maybe they're going through that now.

I can counsel a lot of women who've lost their husbands because I've been through it. I can counsel people who've lost babies because I've been through it. I can counsel people who've lost a lot of money from scams because I've been through it and that's okay.

Those experiences I'm grateful for now that they're in the past and I know that I'm going to have opportunities for growth in the future, but the older I get, the more I realize that we're going to get through these problems and hopefully if they're really bad, you want to get through them quickly. You have to believe that there is a reason they're happening and you've got to learn from it.

There's my daily life. Learn from my good times, learn from my bad times and just try to move forward.

Christy – Debby, as always you're amazing and fabulous and the more we continue to uncover what you've been through, it just solidifies and validates how awesome you are today. It's because of the stuff you've overcome in your past and a lot of times people don't realize you become a champion by overcoming challenges. It's not just a medal you're given to participate. You have to go through something and conquer it

Chapter 3

Without A Vision People Perish
Keshelle Davis
Video – www.bit.ly/manifestdreams-Keshelle

Keshelle Davis is an educator, author, entrepreneur, trainer, and trailblazer. A Master Dreamer and Law of Attraction enthusiast, Keshelle has used it to create the life that she desires and the one she's living right now. For the past five years, she's hosted Dreamboard parties in the Bahamas, teaching attendees how to use the Law of Attraction and other universal principles to create and attract the life they desire. She's also one of Nassau Guardian's Top 40 Under 40 and she's well known for her ability to inspire and empower others.

Keshelle, besides what we've read about you in your bio, tell us more about yourself.

Keshelle – You've seen the professional accolades. I'm a trainer and an entrepreneur, going on 16 years. It's my passion, my love, and my life is training and development groups. But I'm a mother of a beautiful 16-year-old and wife of my wonderful husband. I live in the beautiful Bahamas, in paradise, and get to do what I love each and every day.

Christy – When you talk about the Law of Attraction, Holly touched on it as well, we talked about being in the fire or being in the pit, and then focusing. The day that you decide to take care of yourself is the day that you decide that your life is going to be different.

You have to focus on the dream. You have to focus on the future. You have to focus on something bigger than yourself and then have faith and hold on to that until you become that. Is that what Law of Attraction is?

Keshelle – Yes. It's really about being able to focus on something bigger than yourself. We tend to look at our present circumstances, our present needs, or our present environment. If you're not careful, you can get comfortable there. So being able to look at a mutual desire that's bigger than you, that may seem, near impossible in some cases. Holding on to that and really just having the desire to accomplish whatever it is that you want to accomplish.

Then, of course, having the mindset and the belief that it's possible.

Christy – A lot of times when we're professionals and leaders, we spend a lot of time focusing on other people. We're always focused on what makes other people happy, but we're not necessarily focused on what makes us happy.

What are two things you can give our readers to shift their focus from where they are today, to where they want to be in the future by giving themselves permission to dream about doing something different?

Keshelle – You said it. They have to give themselves permission. It seems simple, but a lot of people allow themselves to believe and live the life they choose. Once they believe it's possible, it may seem like a pie in the sky theory, but it really boils down to getting very clear.

I host my dream board parties here in the Bahamas because getting clear is being able to visualize a picture clearly of what you want in life. You may not have a vision board, but it's something that I highly recommend.

Sometimes it's just taking 15-20 minutes a day to dream, to imagine, to wish. Put yourself out of your current environment regardless of how it may seem or how it looks and really dream. Allow yourself to dream.

I had a dream board party recently and one of the women was having a difficult time writing what she wanted. I told her, "Ask yourself the question, IF this was possible," because she couldn't believe it was possible. She had such limiting beliefs. I said, "Imagine yourself if it was possible, what would you dream?"

Being able to give yourself permission to dream, and giving yourself time to write out, draw out and visualize what it is that you truly want.

Christy – I love talking to you about dreaming and the Law of Attraction. When I was at my desk, at 11 pm on a Friday, I would want to beat myself up, but I would lean back in my chair and say, "When I retire, I want my office to be outside. I don't want to work for anyone. I want to be an entrepreneur, I don't care what I'm selling."

I started to list off 10 things that I wanted and it almost became this mantra that every time I got in a tough spot, I would visualize that life and that is The Life that I live today. Four years ago, that was ridiculous. It was not going to happen. You talked about a vision board and I have a vision board as well.

Talk about the vision board and speaking your vision, and what are two steps that our readers can take?

Keshelle – You have to focus. I do a lot of coaching and mentorship with clients and one of the things that happens so very easily and so very quickly, I do an activity called The Reality Check. Which really gives you an opportunity to sit down and ask yourself some tough questions about where you are right now as it relates to where you want to be. It can get very depressing for some people.

I also do it in my own life when things get tough or when I get some bad news or when things want to derail me. Focus on the vision. That's number one. Focus on the vision and that vision has to be inspiring. It has to even be fearful. Be afraid of it, that means that it's big enough for you and for it to be able to pull you.

Secondly, after the vision, you have to be able to develop the strategy and the plan. I do a seminar called "The 12 Keys - 12 Steps To Making Your Dream A Reality." That covers important steps like being able to have the right people and how people can influence your vision and your dream. Focus on the provision to be able to make that vision a reality and several other steps.

Being able to focus on the vision when things get tough and then be able to have that step by step blueprint, and that plan of ACTION to make it a reality.

Christy – Action is definitely an important piece and I go back to what Napoleon Hill said about opportunity, I love Napoleon Hill. In one of my favorite quotes, he said, "Opportunity takes the sly back door approach and it usually shows up in the form of work. Which is why most people don't recognize opportunity when it comes."

You just talked about having a vision, getting clear and writing it down, and then taking action. Once you're moving forward, you'll see opportunity because you know where you're going. So when that door gets knocked on, you're like, "Oh my God, it just happened for me."

Talk to us about opportunity and how when you're clear on where you're going, you'll know when it shows up.

Keshelle – You hit my favorite words, "You'll know." I'm known as an entrepreneur in the Bahamas, so when people want to make that big leap, from employee to entrepreneur, and I've done it some many times, I tend to be the one that they find and the question that I get often is, "How do you know when to leverage an opportunity or to go after an opportunity to start a business?" Or whatever the dream is.

In a lot of cases, my answer is, you just know. We all know when the time is right and there are cases when the time isn't right and you feel that you need to make that move.

Being able to have that clarity. Clarity does not come from thinking. Clarity comes from action. I can't sit here or you can't sit here and think about the vision or write that plan and say "I'm going to get clear," without taking the steps to move towards that goal or vision. The more steps that you take, even if it's the wrong steps, but the steps that you take that's closer to the goal or the vision creates the clarity. Clarity comes from action. Clarity comes from movement and a lot of people fail to realize that.

Christy – I have people who say, "I'm going to quit my job tomorrow and God is going to show up."

He doesn't work like that. If you don't have a sense of where you want to be and where you're going and who you want to become and how you're going to serve…there's homework that needs to be done before you get to that point. You're looking for a miracle, but a miracle comes when you're prepared for opportunity.

I think about when I met a guy with a network marketing company, a coffee company, he was so happy. I looked and said, "I don't care if he's selling wrenches."

After two weeks with that company, I saw they were all happy. A lot of people in network marketing are highly personally developed. They have drive. When you're seeking something and you're seeking purpose, there is a lightness that you have. There is a different type of determination because you're serving other people.

When I saw him, he was annoyingly happy. I thought, "Who walks around that freaking happy all day?" But I was secretly wanting to be him, in that spirit and lightness because I was in so much pain at the time and after two weeks, I thought about it and asked, "Is this what I've been praying for?"

I thought God would move me in my career because I had nearly four years left to get a full pension and this coffee company… It's a coffee company and I'm a leader. This coffee company is not within that career path and I eventually made the decision to jump and that's the thing when it comes to opportunity because I was clear on how I wanted to feel.

I was clear on how I wanted my life to be and when I was exposed to people who had exactly what I wanted, it was showing me. I'm going to work, I'm miserable. I'm hanging out with these coffee people and they're all happy. I had to take action. That's what you talked about.

Keshelle – It goes to the environment and that's a big part about accomplishing the life that you want to accomplish. Who's influencing those actions, those activities, those beliefs, those mindsets?

To say that you have a vision or a goal, and you're not putting yourself amongst people who are moving also on their visions and goals, eventually your steam, your spark will go away.

When I left my good government job, my first leap, I've done many leaps. I think it was my first leap into entrepreneurship full-time, leaving my good government job as a single mother, with little money in the bank, but I had a vision and I had a dream and I had a desire and all those things we talked about.

But one of the things I felt very strongly about, and I felt secure about, even when making such an uncertain step in my life. I had support. I had the right people around me that said to me, "Keshelle, go after your dreams, go after your vision. Whatever happens, we're here to support you."

That's a critical part of the process in pursuing whatever it is that you're pursuing. Make sure that you have one person. Someone who, in addition to yourself, believes in YOU. Sometimes we tend to want to have people who believe in our vision. It may not happen right away, but people who believe in you, and believe that whatever it is that you're doing and whatever it is that you believe in, they're there to support. That goes a long, long way.

Christy – Share your insight on "those" people. When I think about when I wanted to go, there were 2 people out of 200 that gave support to the lunacy. I was hurt a lot in realizing that the other 198 were not necessarily for me.

Tell the readers about separating themselves from the people who may not be the people that will accompany them on the next journey of their life.

Keshelle – There's a book called, *What Got You Here Won't Get You There*, and it's such a true statement as it relates to everything in your life when you're moving and growing.

When it comes to people, my philosophy is, "I am allergic to negative people." For a purpose-minded individual, for a person with a vision, dream, and a particular goal, you have to get a very very low tolerance. If possible, zero tolerance with people who don't support or who try to negate what it is you're trying to do.

I don't know who that is because I don't allow it. I've heard people say, "I don't have the right environment." Then change your environment. A lot of my friends talk about spending time with people you can trust and people who support you. Who can say, "Yay!"

Christy, you do it quite a lot of times, just support and celebrate people. If you can't find one or two people who celebrate you...Christy you found two. Many people may not be able to find two so easily. You have to find another circle. You have to find another set of associations and it may very well be a difficult thing to move away from people who love you or who's in your current circle, but in order to get to the next level, you must.

There is a quote, you are the sum total of the people you surround yourself with and the books that you read. It's become a cliché now for most people, but it's such a true statement. If you look around your circle and you're not happy with the lifestyles of the people around you and their lifestyle isn't something that you aspire to, then it's a good time to change your circle.

I'll share a quick story. Last year I was at a serious place where I had outgrown my circle. I love my girlfriends, and they are still my girlfriends, but I really had poured so much into personal development and professional development.

I'm a constant learner and I looked around and thought, "I love these girls, and we're all striving, but I'm not growing anymore in this circle."

I really made the conscious decision to uplevel my associations. That didn't mean I had to disassociate with my current circle, but I intentionally found a new group, an additional group to be in.

That's really how we met Christy, because shortly after that I found my way to Sharon Lecther's event and I could relate to the level of women to uplevel with. It was amazing. It blew my mind and I was saying to my coach how afraid I was moving so fast and she reminded me. She said, "Keshelle, a few months earlier you said that you outgrew your circle and now you're saying you can't keep up."

So it's just being aware of who you're surrounding yourself with. You can love them to death, but you can also love them in other ways, but you have to be in a place where you put yourself around people who pull you, stretch you, can support you and cheer you on. If you don't have that already, it's the first thing you should add to your list of things to do.

Christy – I want to talk about upleveling. As you talked about finding another circle and not being around people without the lifestyles you desire, I think about my circle. We were successful. We all made six-figures. We all had multiple degrees and the accoutrements of success, but I still wanted more. We are sometimes made to feel guilty about it, especially from some people who consider that to be their pinnacle.

You're going to get resistance from people who feel this should be good enough and why aren't you happy with what you have. Even though we're unhappy with what should make us happy.

When I think about leaving that group and it took three years to meet the level of women we had in the room at Sharon Lechter's event. Also to meet you, as you remind me a lot of my younger self. I never knew that people existed who were like me. Who had that drive, who had that determination, so to leave that group of friends behind and find a group of people who were exactly what I wanted.

It was scary and I didn't talk for the first two days, and I talk A LOT! I started talking on the third day, but people can still see success in you, even if you don't say anything. To this day, that group of women blew my mind because I had never been around so many powerful women before, and there were a few great men too.

I started talking on the third day because I had become comfortable in the group and was happy to be around women who were just as relentless as me. That's why I say you remind me a lot about myself because you are just as relentless, and a little...I won't call you crazy because you like to jump, but you do have to be crazy to jump. I had never met another woman who shared similar power, which is how we became good friends.

You've shared insight on upleveling and lifestyle, what advice do you have for our readers to find the light in the midst of their storm?

Keshelle – You have to recognize that storms will come. Not if they come, but when they come. You have to realize that's a part of the whole process, so it really releases the surprise factor.

Secondly, one of my favorite sayings by John Maxwell, "You lose or you learn." Recognize that whatever challenges you go through, regardless of how it comes and we all have our challenges.

I remember my first year in business, my car got repossessed three times. I don't think I've shared that story with you. You look for the lesson in everything that you go through and always focus on the vision. Look for the lesson, focus on the vision.

Ask yourself what is the greatest lesson, because if you don't find that lesson very quickly or spend time focusing on the lesson, you may end up repeating that challenge; whatever it is. Look for the lesson, so when tough times come, focus on the vision, which means you must have the vision in the first place. Being able to get clear. Look for the lesson, focus on the vision.

Christy – I think you were being lenient on saying you *may* get that test again, I was thinking, "No, you *will* get that test again."

Keshelle – Yes. Yes, you will.

Christy – When you're looking for that lesson and asking, "What can I learn from this?" You'll see that you've been down this road before and then you'll think that you've almost been taught this lesson five times and then you still don't realize it.

On the sixth or twentieth time, or the hundredth time when it shows up again, you now have an opportunity to change what you didn't do the first time and then you'll see that you will move to the next lesson, right?

Keshelle – Yes. Just like school, if you don't pass the first test, you'll more than likely have to take that test again and again and again until you pass it. Life is the same way.

Christy – Keshelle, I love spending time with you. Thank you so much for sharing your insight again with the readers. Dr. Munroe lives on through you!

Chapter 4

From Refugee to Renaissance Woman
Dr. Emily Letran
Video – www.bit.ly/manifestdreams-Emily

Dr. Emily Letran is a business mentor, speaker, author, philanthropist and business owner of two multi-specialty group practices. She published, *From Refugee to Renaissance Woman*, and shares her experience when she arrived in the US as a 13-year-old refugee. With relentless persistence, inner strength, and self-confidence, she's been able to overcome adversity and blaze a trail for generations to come. She's been featured as a TEDx speaker and is a testament that dreams do come true with hard work and a mission of serving others.

Emily, besides what we just read about you in your bio, tell us more about yourself.

Emily – I would want to claim that I'm the best mom in the world, according to my children, because I'm claiming it myself. I'm dedicated to the family and put family first. I operate on integrity and one of the missions that I'm on is to help people get rid of the entitlement mentality.

I want people to understand what it takes to be successful, and it's not about other people helping you. It's really about you helping yourself get to the next level by your clarity, your commitment and your decision to make changes every day and living your life with intentions.

Christy – You just talked about living your life with intention, what do you mean by that? A lot of people don't understand what it means to be on purpose or live with intention. Can you expand on that concept?

Emily – For me, living with intention is knowing where you want to go and what you want to achieve. For example, if you have a business and you say, "I'm running this business to make money."

That may be a good goal, but what is the ultimate intention. What do you want to accomplish besides providing for your family?

In my case, I'm a dentist and High Performance Coach. With a dental practice, I'm providing services to the community and of course, that helps me provide for my family. The intention there is actually to change lives. Not just doing dentistry and making money, but it changes lives because what I do affects other people.

If I give an older gentleman a beautiful smile, he'll be able to go home and share that smile with his family and create beautiful memories. Even though I'm just working on his teeth, I'm touching his family also.

The intention there is really to change lives, not just getting you a set of teeth that you can smile and chew food with. The same thing with any position or job that people have. They may be showing up eight hours and getting a paycheck, but what is the ultimate purpose? Is it your mortgage? You're putting hours in, but you really are helping to change lives.

Someone buying a house, getting a mortgage from you. That's a big milestone. So, when people think of their work in that sense, they can see there is a bigger purpose in life in what they do. That would typically give people the inspiration to do their best and to really excel in what they do. Versus saying, "I'm going to come in and do my eight hours and I just want my commission check when I close the mortgage."

That can become a mundane task, something that you do day in and day out. You no longer have the passion for it, because, after a while, it's just a "job" and you don't see the impact it has for your clients. That's what I mean about intention.

Christy – I agree. Dr. Myles Munroe said something like, "To have a big house and drive a fancy car, that's not purpose, that's ambition."

Purpose is about serving others, so if you think that your purpose is going to be used specifically for you, that's not your purpose. Your purpose is using your gifts to impact other people.

Emily – Right. Once I learned that, I see that I'm a dentist and I have two offices and I'm in southern California, so what else can I do? How can I impact people more beyond the location of the dental offices? That is one of the reasons I started my Foundation because one of the goals of the Foundation is to raise money where we can get a mobile dental unit, so we can go out further to help and do community outreach. It will be beyond where I'm located in my city. One of the ambitions is to encourage dentists in other communities to provide that type of service in their communities.

That way, we won't just go to work in our office, we can reach out more. It's a brick and mortar business and sometimes you think you're limited to your location, but when you think about it a little more, you can do more. I reach out to other dentists and encourage them to do one free day of dentistry a year in their practice. Give back to the community. When you do that, you feel better and all of a sudden, you find your purpose to change people's lives.

It's not just, "I'm going to work from 9-6 and I'm going to make X dollars and then go home and buy whatever I need for my family."

That will become repetitious and over time if you don't have purpose, you will lose that passion.

Christy – Share with the readers about people who say they're at a disadvantage because they didn't go to private school. They don't have the accoutrements of success. Their parents didn't have this or they weren't allowed to do that. Tell us more, including your story, that if you have the vision and the will and if you work hard, anything is possible for anyone.

Emily – Thank you for asking me that. I believe that everyone has a story. You may not realize you have a story until you sit down and start writing your own story. Then you realize I do have a story. I have a journey.

When I first came to this country, I didn't have anything. We came, basically empty handed, as refugees. We stayed with our cousin who had been here a couple of years before that. The money that we received was from the government, because of the refugee status. I always went to public school. I received free lunch at school because there was six of us and everyone was under 16 years old and we went to live with my aunt, who was a single parent.

We got those kind of benefits from the government and I would credit a lot of what I've achieved to reading. You're reading about people who have achieved a lot of things. When I was much younger, one of my favorites was Madam Curie. She went through a lot of hardships and got the Nobel Prize. Those kinds of individuals that when you look at how successful they are and then look back, they had a story. Another person was Billy Preston, he had challenges too. They all had their ups and downs.

When you read about those people, you get inspired. You feel where you are is not necessarily what you have to be. You can change and that's done through reading.

The other thing is to have an open mind. One of the things that I still do, but it used to motivate me, I would look at a friend who was driving a car in high school because his mom and dad gave him a car. He looks like me. He's in my same class. I probably have a better grade. How could he have certain things and the mentality is, if we're similar and if he can do it and get it, I can do it too.

Be open minded, instead of looking at him and saying there's no way I can get to that level because he has the right parents. I'm not looking at him because of his family, I'm just looking at me and him. You're comparing just yourself to the other person, and you're not going to lump in all the circumstances.

He comes from a rich background, but me and him, his abilities, his potential and my abilities, my potential. If we're similar, and he can achieve more, then I need to at least give it a try and get to his level.

As I raise my kids, right now we live in a pretty affluent community. Not because I'm affluent, but because we got lucky and bought the house For Sale By Owner. When I got to that community, everyone was shocked and said, "That's where all the rich people live."

I didn't care that's where all the rich people lived. I wanted the house in that community for the school district for my kids. That was the only reason. It has nothing to do with rich people, because at that point, I had two offices and basically everything I do, besides taking care of the family, it goes back to paying the loan.

I'm not rich. I know I can be, if I work and pay off my loans. I have my kids there and they go to public school in a good area. I teach them the values of what you have, doing the most and making the best out of what you already have. You don't need things handed to you, whether it's from rich grandparents or whoever.

This is what I tell my kids and they don't like it very much, I tell them I do have money, I just don't give it to you.

Christy – LOL!

Emily – I think I heard that from Dr. Huxtable or Clair Huxtable. I tell them if you want to know if mom has money or not, look at the office and see if mom can buy whatever it is for the office, maybe some high tech thing. That's where the money goes because it's an investment for the business, which will generate money, but mom doesn't have money to take you on a two-week cruise to Europe.

It's where I choose to put my money because I can see where I put my money is an investment. Whenever we decide to take a cruise, that's a different story.

You show that to the people around you, whether it's your kids or employees. You spend the money where you think it will generate the most benefit for you to step up. It's not for you just to enjoy right now....let's go and eat a $500 dinner. That's something that I don't think I will most likely never do, because with $500, I can put that into some type of investment.

That goes back to the intention. What do you want to do with your life? What do you want to do with your everyday activities? Because if you already have that intention and that goal, whether you have money or an opportunity that comes in, you know exactly what to do with it. But if you don't, it will just be, okay, let me see what I can do.

With me, if I got an extra hour because my patient canceled, I know exactly what I'm going to do with that hour because I have a purpose. Today I need to do XYZ and an extra hour is going to be allocated to an activity that I planned on doing tomorrow. If that time slot opens, I'm going to do something else.

If we all plan what we want to do with our life and we have a clear intention, sometimes it doesn't come right away. For me, it comes with the reading, being open-minded, and to be mentored or to learn from experts. Because we don't know everything. The way I do it, I look at the mentor, see what the mentor does with their free time.

They're still busy, but sometimes they're busy going to a charity event, rather than being busy going shopping, because you're busy too, you go shopping. It's an activity that occupies your time, but what does it do for you and does it fit in with your intention and your purpose?

Christy – Once you get clear on who you are and where you're going, you'll know exactly what to do with your time and money and how you want to feel. So many people get caught up on making other people feel good about them and they go to activities, like a two-week cruise, even if they have to stay up for the next two months trying to figure out how they're going to pay for it.

Going on these expensive vacations, and buying these cars and homes that don't necessarily serve them, but it looks good to other people. Living in purpose and with intention is about how things *feel good to you* and not about making other people *feel good about you*.

Emily – Right. It has to do with clarity. You need to know yourself. If I'm going to follow and keep up with the Joneses and they're not me, after a while, I'm going to be lost. If I had that much stuff or that much money, I wouldn't know what to do with myself unless I'm clear on what I want to do.

If people are all about material things, that's where they're going to put all their money, energy and time to acquire those. I'm not like that and if I try to copy them, after a certain amount of time, I'm going to be lost because I won't know myself.

I think it's very important for people to know themselves first. They need to know where they're coming from, what's important to them, their values and their beliefs. Whether it's family, status or income because status and income sometimes don't go together.

You can have an empty title and you may not be making the money. I'm very much about substance and being practical. You can tell me about whatever is out there that's flashy, and fancy and it doesn't appeal to me because I'm so clear about myself. I will refuse to change for those types of things.

I would encourage the readers to really get to know themselves first. Then you can go out and learn about other people, other things, other mentors. That's why when we're coaching people, we need to help them get clear on what they want. Because if they aren't clear, you can coach people all day long and keep refiguring out what they want, because they aren't clear.

Christy – What are two or three questions that people can ask themselves to get to know themselves a little better? I ask this question because when I resigned from my career and someone asked me what would make me happy, I was shocked because I didn't know.

I didn't know what would make me happy, but I knew what would make the 20 people around me happy, but no one ever asked me what would make me happy, which is why I was unhappy. I was shocked, but more disappointed that I had not given that same attention and effort to what made me happy.

Then it became a journey and discovery of who am I and I learned that I lost myself so much along the way based on what was considered normal by society. We'll never be normal.

Again, what are two or three questions that people can ask themselves to get to know themselves a little better?

Emily – One of the questions that my coaches ask is, "If money was no object, what activity would you want to do?" It has nothing to do with money. What do you want to do? If people can answer that, and it can get clearer with time, but if they can answer that, it will usually point the person to where their passion is. If it's your passion, you will tend to lean towards that, regardless of the money. That's one question someone can ask themselves, "If it wasn't about money, what would I rather do?"

For me, in the recent years, philanthropy is the one that keeps popping up. I'm working and trying to pay back my business loans because I had three offices at one point, and sometimes you deal with work challenges where someone quits and wants to sue you.

But when I asked myself the question, it always goes back to charity and philanthropy. That's where I think, okay my purpose in life at this point is going to be that. Although I have 20 other things that I have to deal with, that's going to be my purpose at this point.

The other thing that people can ask themselves, which is a question that a coach asked me, I was doing several things at the time and she said, "Pick one thing that you want to do."

I said I can't really pick one and she said, "If I were going to roll you down a cliff right now and you can only do one thing, what would it be?"

I got clear right away because you can only do one thing and you got to pick one. It really goes back to what your values are, and what's important to you. For example, what's really important to me is my family, but with time, when the kids grow up, they're going to leave the house, so you don't have a big family anymore. So, what am I going to do to fill up my time?

That's one of the reasons I decided to do coaching. First of all, I wanted to help people gain the knowledge that I've already gained from learning from other coaches and mentors. Two, I want to get rid of the entitlement mentality. I don't want to hear the excuses I can't do this, it's too hard and I don't know where you find the time.

Everyone has 24 hours. I don't know why, but between me and my friends, I'm the one with the most time. I have no idea how. I want to help people get clarity and decide, of the 20 activities that you do, which 10 are most important and then just drop the other 10. Then make time to go and do something that's more beneficial for you.

The third thing is to be able to impact more people. Just like I said with the dentistry, the dentistry is more local. If I want to have a mobile unit, I can drive it around, but it's still going to be limited in the distance. If I'm doing coaching, I can be in California, but still help someone across the country.

I can see myself potentially reaching more people and changing more lives with that and I think that will help fill in the void of not having the family or with the kids. You just grow a larger community that will become your family. They're not your blood relatives, but they will become your family and in that sense, it's still about family, but it's more community and it's about helping each other get to the next level. Which is exactly what you do with your family.

Those are the questions that people can ask themselves. When they ask themselves that, they need to be clear about their values. Because if you're not sure what your values are, then when you ask that question, sometimes it's very difficult to answer.

Christy – In the book, *Happier,* by Tal Ben Shahar, he talked about the definition of happiness. I didn't really know I was unhappy until I saw his model. What does happiness really mean? When he gave the framework, I was like, "You know what? I'm not happy!"

He said to write down the hours that you're doing certain things. Most of us are Rat Racers, we are in present detriment for a future benefit. We are working right now to retire, so we're giving up our happiness in this moment for a future benefit.

He asked what are some of the things that you like to do now? You can do those things in the present to offset your unhappiness because you're a rat racer. I like to mentor people, so instead of watching tv or working really late, I would go and talk to high school students.

This offset the unhappiness of that present moment because I was doing what I liked to do. That was one of the things you mentioned. A lot of people don't think they have time to do anything different from what they're doing, but if they can track some of the activities that aren't giving them the happiness they want, they should stop doing those and do something they actually like which is attached to their values.

Emily – Sometimes, when people have limiting beliefs, they think they can only do so much and that's because they've been doing it for many years. If they do that and they don't look outside, they don't keep an open mind. They think that's the only option or the only way. They're just going to continue on that path.

I can't tell you how many self-improvement seminars that I go to and I would see people who just retired and they're there to learn and it always inspires me because they're older than me. Someone who's 70 and he's there to learn. He wants to start another career. It's so inspiring.

I was at a seminar one time learning to place implants and I'm not interested in placing implants. That's a surgery and I don't love surgery, but I wanted to take the class to learn what's involved. I was sitting next to this doctor and his hair was all white. I know he's older, probably 70 something, and he looked at me and asked, "How do you like the class?"

I said, "It just confirmed that I don't like surgery."

I asked him, "How do you like the class?"

He said, "It's pretty nice."

I then asked, "What do you like to practice?"

He said he was an orthodontist. If you know orthodontists, they're the braces people. They don't do surgery at all. Actually, the assistants do the work most of the time. The orthodontist is more of the brainwork and plans how they're going to move the teeth.

I was really shocked. Looking at this man in his 70's, I then asked why he taking this class because it has nothing to do with him. He said, "Because I want to learn."

I was in awe of someone like that because he doesn't deal with surgery, and probably hasn't since he graduated from ortho school and he's there to learn. Then I went home and talked to a friend and she doesn't have any time at all and thinks she knows everything.

It's so frustrating and that's why I wanted to do coaching because I figured, why don't I just start with people around me and change them if they want to change. It's actually not that hard. Instead of watching tv for an hour, read a book for an hour and that can cause a shift. You're still spending an hour entertaining your brain, but in a good way. Sometimes if I want to entertain myself, I'll sit there and watch tv for an hour.

On Thursday evening, I watch tv three hours straight.

Christy – I know what you're watching. Lol!

Emily – You know what, that's me and my son. That's our time. We watch Scandal, then Grey's Anatomy, then How to Get Away With Murder. I'm usually lost before the third show is on. But, that's our night, Thursday night, me and him. He's 13 years old.

Of course, the shows are interesting, but I'm really doing it for him. It doesn't mean that I don't watch tv or late night shows, but again going back to what I said earlier, you need to put an intention.

If I say, okay I just want to waste an hour right now, well yeah, I'm just going to sit here and watch tv, not really searching for something. If I want to study marketing, I may still watch tv for an hour, but I'll be watching infomercials. Not to buy stuff, but to listen to the words they use.

I just went to a marketing seminar over the weekend and the trainer told us to try to sell a 16-18" diamond cut gold chain with cubic zirconia. He said, this is what we're trying to sell and went into this lavish discussion of what this chain can do for you to make you feel like, "Oh, I want to buy the chain now!"

That's what I mean when you're watching an infomercial, but if you're watching with the intention of "I want to know what they're saying to get people to buy," you're going to get something from that. They're not selling anything real fancy, but they motivate and get people to buy it. So you can watch an infomercial with the intention to learn what they're saying or you can just sit there and watch it so you can buy something.

Christy – Emily, thank you so much for your insight! I always enjoy spending time with you and squeezing your brain for whatever nuggets will come out of it. I'm sure our reader have enjoyed your insight as well and will use it to set better intentions in their life.

Chapter 5

Using Corporate Experience To Fuel Destiny
Debra Banks
Video – www.bit.ly/manifestdreams-Debra

Debra Banks is the Founder of TNC Business Consulting (The Numbers Count). She supports businesses and coaches people in improving their operations and increasing profits. For over 30 years, she's used numbers to grow corporate departments, built her own businesses and generated millions of dollars in sales for her team and others. After building a successful and proven model, Debra stepped out of her comfort zone last year and is working to exponentially expand her business while working her corporate job.

Debra, besides what we just read about you in your bio, tell us more about yourself.

Debra – I have two formal degrees and a Ph.D. from the school of hard knocks. My formal degrees are a B.S. in Business and an MBA, both from the University of Virginia. After getting my degrees, I was able to use that college training in various corporate jobs. I've worked for very large Fortune 500 companies in different areas of marketing, business, finance, accounting, operations.

I've also run a couple of businesses in between various corporate stints. So I've had that great experience of working in corporations and understanding the principles of how large corporations run their businesses and I used those principles when I ran my small businesses.

About a year ago, I saw a void in the market. I moved to Florida and joined a couple of organizations looking to connect with various people. I saw there were a lot of small business owners who were missing out on the opportunity to understand what large corporations do and how they can use it in their small business.

TNC Business Consulting has been an awesome opportunity to use my formal education, experience, and education from the school of hard knocks to assist and support other business owners in using those principles to improve their process. It's been great.

Christy – Debra, you're unique from the other ladies featured in this book, because you're still working your successful corporate job while building your business on the side. Tell us about purpose and what it means to you.

Debra – I am very fortunate that my corporate position still gives me purpose. Working for a very large insurance company, I'm constantly learning new ways to look at business. New ways to present and so I'm able to thrive and be on purpose in my corporate job. However, I saw that some small businesses were not benefitting from those principles, so I can live on purpose when I work with clients in the evenings and on the weekend.

It's been very rewarding for me to take my education, take what I do for large corporations and use that to support small businesses. It's been powerful to help small business owners see how their vision, their mission, and their passion can be turned into profits because often people are doing things that aren't profitable. I focus on the numbers and talk about how we can take their vision and passion and turn it into profits.

Christy – For some people, purpose involves leaving their careers. Keshelle Davis worked in banking, now she's an entrepreneur, a trainer and does other large events. Your purpose involves numbers, and you said your career is rewarding. You found purpose in your career and in your small business with serving other people, right?

Debra – They are aligned from the standpoint that I'm taking the principles I used, learned, and experienced in a large corporation and breaking those down and showing small businesses how they can use the principles in their business, so there's complete alignment.

Being a numbers person, I focus on my own numbers. I'm building a business that has the trajectory of replacing my income. It is a solid, thought through plan of how I can apply myself. I use what I'm learning every day in my corporate job to assist other business owners, so it's complete alignment. To be honest, it's also aligned with my goal to not work with clients in desperation.

I can be selective and work with those clients who are ready because I have limited time. I find that I waste less time. I'm very efficient with my time because I am allocating it between my full-time job and my business.

It's really building efficiency within me, so when I'm coaching and consulting with other coaches and business owners, it create efficiencies within them because it's something that I'm living. I see some of my clients wasting time because they have it, and I'm very efficient with dollars and time.

Christy – You talked about being selective. If your primary means of income is your corporate job, you can be selective in some regards because as entrepreneurs, sometimes our money gets real funny. Sometimes you have to take what comes, so standing on a higher ground and being selective with who you take, that's awesome.

Debra – It's more rewarding for me to work with people who are ready and have a clear vision of what it is they want. The clients that I work with are very clear. Sometimes when you're coaching or consulting it can take a lot of time to try to motivate folks. I can set up expectations of what it is to work with me and those folks who are willing to step up to the plate and are really ready to move forward, and hear the tough lessons and the tough words that I have around looking at the numbers. This helps them understand the viability of their business.

I just keep it real and sometimes I have to say to folks that the business model they're creating is not one that's viable. Then those opportunities where the business model is viable, we can take off.

I recently worked with a client who had gone from $0, to knowing where various investors were vying to invest up to $500,000 in her business based on the business model and the financial model that we did. It's very rewarding to work with people who are ready to move ahead.

One of my favorite lines is in the movie *Jerry McGuire*, where he said, "Show me the money. Show me the money." I always say, if you're a business owner and you want to show me the money, then you need to show me the numbers. Without numbers, without an understanding of what it takes to create a profit, then you're not in business until you make that leap.

For many business owners, it's okay, but it all depends on what your objective is. There are some business owners who really don't have a strong need to earn a lot in their business. That's not the case for me. I am the sole provider for myself and have a home and lifestyle that I want to keep, so my business has to make a certain amount of money in order to meet my financial needs. For people who are really serious about their business, it has to be about the numbers. So show me the numbers.

Christy – One question with regards to working on your job and then working in your small business. Is there a line that you draw? I don't want to beat a dead horse here, but are the feelings different when you're working on your job and when you're working in your purpose, or is it all the same? How does that feel for you?

Debra – It's definitely more living in purpose when I'm working with small business owners because when you work for a large corporation, your impact is not felt as strongly. I work with an organization with over 30,000 employees, so although my contributions are still working on purpose, it's just a piece of the puzzle.

When I'm working with small business owners, both my contributions and theirs is felt strongly, because they have a small team of people. Even if they have a medium size group of people, it has more impact.

What we do together certainly has more impact. The feeling is different. The principles are the same. The satisfaction of seeing results and seeing changes are different because you can see the needle move more in a small company. It's been very rewarding. The clients I work with, when what we do together has a direct impact on the quality of life of their family, it's much more rewarding.

Christy – What advice do you have for readers who are currently working in their jobs, and although they like their jobs, they also see themselves branching out to serve people. You saw a gap in the market and you have the skills to fill it. What advice do you have for readers to shift to a small business based on what their gifts are while working in their corporate jobs?

Debra – Being on purpose or being on passion is based on doing something that you love. Sometimes my friends will say you work a lot, but I really don't consider it work. My advice would be to do something that you love to do. I know you hear it all the time, but it's so true. I know I'm a little different from a lot of folks because I actually like doing Excel spreadsheets.

I like looking at the power of the numbers and creating a profitable business, and changing the numbers, what if we did this and what if scenarios. Seeing folk's eyes light up when you create a five-year plan and see where the business could go.

Sometimes you meet people who are in a job and they're trying to think of something to do on the side, but the closer you can be aligned with really loving something, then it will be easier to devote your evenings and weekends to something, because otherwise it will be very very tiring to work all day and then work on the weekends and evenings on something you didn't love to do and that you're not good at. My advice is to find something that you love to do and that you're bringing value to.

Christy – What trainings or workshops have you attended that gave you clarity on continuing to build your business?

Debra – The actual mechanics of what I do, which is the Excel spreadsheets, I've already been trained on that. I've attended several online and in-person courses on marketing and sales, and training on speakers. I've adopted the notion that the better you can convey clarity and confidence around what you're doing, you can attract new folks to want to work with you.

I've attended several sessions on speaking. I have a coach and attend online training. I'm a perpetual student, but I don't want to overdue on the learning. I want to do. I have a good combination of learning and doing.

Christy – What have you learned about yourself in this process of building, besides being efficient? Are there any other things you've learned about yourself and any advice you can give readers on what they may learn about themselves as they step out and learn how to work more in their passion, in addition to working their jobs.

Debra – The thing that I've learned about myself is to pace myself and be patient. Also, to trust the universe that the right thing will happen at the right time. About a year and a half ago, I was in a rush to make things happen and got involved with a particular business that was not in alignment and not in my passion, because I thought it would get me out of my corporate position more quickly. When I found something that I loved to do, and that I'm great at, I pace myself accordingly and allow the universe to let opportunities come.

That's when more things happen. It's really been a great lesson for me to see that I don't have to rush things. I just move forward one step at a time and it all seems to come to fruition.

Christy – Some of the points you made are key because you talked about pacing yourself and sometimes people are presented with opportunities and they think they're going to get rich quick. I was one of those people. LOL! Because I was successful in my career, I thought, "How hard can entrepreneurship be?" OMG!

You talked about taking courses on marketing and speaking. There are different skills that are needed for entrepreneurs, which is what we need outside of our jobs, regardless of how successful we think we are.

TD Jakes said, "This…is not that." If you're stepping into a new arena, you're now going to have to rebuild your skills in that arena. Do you agree with what I said earlier about people having the misconception that they can get rich quick because they are successful in other areas?

Debra – That's exactly what I was speaking to. Wanting it to happen more quickly than it happens. It's a great balance because you do want to act. I often run into people who are the opposite, that have the motivation to do something, but they aren't taking the action.

They're focused on feeling good and manifestation, but not on action. It's a balance to pace yourself, but to stay in action and to know that as an employee, there are certain things that you don't have to do, but as an entrepreneur, there are others that you do.

It's always helpful to have a mentor. People that you can learn from because you don't know what you don't know.

Christy – YES!!!

Debra – Until you've been around people who've been there before, of course, you have to be open to listening and learning. It's a journey. It's definitely a journey being an entrepreneur. For the lucky few, although sometimes we think they were lucky and it happened overnight, but many of those overnight sensations really weren't overnight.

It takes time. As an entrepreneur, you try different things and learn as you go. I've even seen that with you as you've grown so much since I met you, by constantly moving forward and getting closer and closer to your purpose and allowing more people to see what you can bring to the world. It just takes time for folks, and patience and pacing really pay off.

Christy – It does and you said something that was great, faith. People have faith, but the Bible says, "Faith without works is dead."

Taking the action. You also said, "You don't know what you don't know."

I remember a couple of years ago, I said I was going to work on something, but before I started, I needed to have 20 things in place. I had a vision and although it was awesome, I didn't know what to do.

Three months later, I noticed that I was no closer to the vision because I didn't take action on it, so I jumped in. I said, "Well I need to figure it out along the way."

When I took action and started to move forward on that vision, I saw the 100 things I had no clue about.

I wish I would have gotten a mentor earlier because they could have told me about the 100 things I didn't know. Mentorship is the key, especially for highly successful people, because we think we know a lot, and it's a lot that we don't know. As an entrepreneur, people take advantage of you for what you don't know.

Debra – Speaking of action, I was having a conversation with Pas Simpson the other day, he said something that was so powerful. Many in the network, and you and some of our friends, really love the book, *Think and Grow Rich*. He said, "Beyond *Think and Grow Rich*, that's good and it makes you rich in thought, but you have to act to become wealthy."

I think some people get stuck. Even when you read the book and move past the thinking part, and you really read more into it and what it takes to grow rich, it's not the thinking alone. It's an awesome title and an awesome book and you can definitely grow rich, but you're going to have to act to become wealthy.

Christy – What action can readers take right now if they're considering starting their own business or consulting business while they work their jobs, to either work themselves out of a job or to supplement their income?

Debra – It's important to not just work *in* your business, but to work *on* your business. Working on your business means you don't just do the things that your business is about. You take the known principles and ways that businesses are run and use them in your business.

You can't just think small. If you're a hat maker, you can't just think about making hats. You need to think about the cost of the material, your marketing strategy and all of that. It's more about working *on* your business in addition to *in* your business. If someone is still working full-time, you need to allot time to both.

One of the pieces of working on your business is to develop a proforma, a sales plan, and a profit and loss projection of what it is that you're expecting to achieve so that you have something to measure against as you move along in your business. So you set up an expectation and you measure what actually happens against what it is that you're expecting to happen.

Christy - Debra, this conversation has been awesome and I hope that the readers will consider working full time in their jobs and part time in their purpose. This will refresh their lives, make them happier and get them closer to living their destiny.

Using Corporate Experience To Fuel Destiny

Chapter 6

Seek Purpose In Your Natural Talents
Shannon McGinnis
Video – www.bit.ly/manifestdreams-Shannon

Shannon McGinnis is a business mentor, founder, and CEO of Organized 4 Success, Inc. She's a certified professional organizer, highly sought after international speaker and the author of two instructional organizing books. Shannon works with executives and entrepreneurs who are overwhelmed by the paper and digital clutter in their office, to transform their chaos into systems that save them time and money. This interview is about purpose and how Shannon got into organizing.

Shannon, besides what we just read about you in your bio, tell us more about yourself.

Shannon – I am a natural born organizer. I've been organized all my life, which is what we'll discuss later. I want to share with everyone who is considering what their purpose is and possibly changing careers that I've been in business for 13 years, but I wasn't always a professional organizer.

In fact, I have my bachelors and Master's degrees in Biology. I'm a third-generation scientist and I never would have considered the career that I have now back when I went to college and was first getting started. You can do whatever you dream of when you have your own business. I want to support people with that vision.

Christy – Although we've been friends for a few years, I didn't know you were a third-generation scientist. Going from being a scientist, majoring in biology and that background, how did you get into organizing? What happened in your childhood that led you to getting where you are today and finding your purpose?

Shannon – A few different things happened to help me find my purpose. My parents got divorced when I was really young, so I was raised by a single mom and we moved around quite a lot. I think I was in five different houses by the time I was in the second grade and I always wanted to know where my things were. So, to unpack and set up was really grounding for me.

The other thing that happened was when I was in my late 20s, I moved and lived in several different states between undergraduate and graduate school. Growing up in New Jersey, I moved to California and just decided I wanted to use the other side of my brain. I had been a left side, with an analytical mindset and I asked, "What do I really want to do with my life and myself?"

I pursued a very spiritual path for a number of years and that led me to my commitment to be of service. For me, I learned that there could be a career in professional organizing. That was a very clear yes for me to be of service to other people. For three years before I started my business, I was a cook at a Tibetan Buddhist retreat center because that was serving my spiritual path and it was also a very clear way to be of service.

I think as we go through life and have different bumps in the road or turns in our path, we realize okay...we're getting more and more clear of what our purpose is. My purpose is to be of service to others and to share my gifts as a professional organizer.

Christy – When you talked about being on a spiritual path, how did that start for you? Do you remember the moment and what exactly is a spiritual path in your words?

Shannon – I would say, there wasn't an exact moment. It was in my late 20's, so on an astrological level you could say it was Saturn returns. It was also a very big period of maturation for me in leaving the east coast and my family, and moving to California where I didn't really know anyone, except the friend of mine that I moved there with.

It really was an introduction by a new acquaintance that led me to a spiritual path that I'd never been exposed to. I'd never been exposed to Hinduism or Buddhism and so I got exposed to both of those in moving to California. There were pieces of both that really resonated with me and sort of answered or gave context to some of the questions about the religious upbringing I had as a child.

Christy – Being on a spiritual journey, do you feel that when you're able to quiet your mind, because that's some of the things that go on with Buddhism and Hinduism, that you were able to hear what your soul was asking you for?

Shannon – Yes. Yes. I love that you brought in the word soul because I don't think I'd ever thought about that before. I had an introduction to meditation, chanting, and yoga and just a completely different spiritual immersion. I also went to India by myself for five months. Just really inundated with the opportunity to have more and more clarity. There's lots of learning there, but also just moments of clarity, not being dictated by outside influences. In having those moments of clarity, I was really able to see what is more of my purpose and how do I want to share it with the world.

Christy – The reason I asked that question is because we're so busy and when we're in jobs that we don't like, we have chaos in our lives. We don't appreciate our family as much and there's so much drama that we can't hear what our soul wants, because it's drowned out by the drama of life. Social media has added to that.

I wanted to make that point because when you moved away from your family, then you started to quiet your mind by meditating and chanting and you started breaking off that negative energy. You were also releasing the expectations of what other people wanted you to do. Then you were able to open yourself to say you wanted to be an organizer. What does your family think about that?

Shannon – They were really supportive. They never questioned me on what is that or can you make a living doing that? There was never any doubt about it and certainly, my parents and my sister would understand it because I've always been very organized, so that would be a no brainer. When I started, it was a new field but it wasn't like I was one of the first professional organizers because there were other organizers 10-15 years before me.

It wasn't until Oprah started talking about it that it got out into mainstream consciousness. People were like, "Oh, we can ask for support to get more organized?"

One of the things that I bring up in sharing I have my bachelors and Masters degrees is that we were never taught to be organized. There are plenty of professionals out there juggling parenting, as well as their professional lives while trying to have a personal life. They've never been taught to be organized and often times people hire me because they're overwhelmed or they want to set a better example for their children.

It's really one of the ways we can ask for support and create some lifestyle changes and new habits for our life.

Christy – I love Oprah! Our outer circumstances or outer lives are a reflection of our inner lives. If you have a junky car, junky house or junky office, then your mindset is also filled with junk. When you start to organize your thoughts, house, car or office, then your thoughts will become more organized. They are a reflection of each other.

Shannon – Yes, I agree and think one of the ways to think about that and reframe it is, my definition of clutter. Whether it's clutter in your car or in your home, or your office, clutter is something you haven't made a decision about. I really work with people to empower them to make the decision. There is a lot of coaching involved to ask them the right question because I'm not going to make the decision for them.

Really getting clear and helping them make those decisions because, yeah you mentioned social media and all other things. We're all just very busy and life feels overwhelming. The more and more delayed decisions you have in your life, the more and more confusion, chaos and clutter are also going to be there.

Christy – Earlier you talked about when you made the decision to become an organizer and your family and your sister thought it would be a no-brainer. I think with our purpose, people can see who we are. We think that if we step out on the path and become who we were meant to be, we will meet resistance, not knowing people see us in that way already.

Shannon – I think you bring up a good point for anyone who's listening and thinking about stepping out on their own and feeling like you might not get that support. Certainly, with my family, no one had ever heard of a professional organizer, so we have to think outside the box. It's not one of those things where you're trying to discover your purpose that you can ask other people what your purpose is because that really comes from within.

But when you develop it, of course, it's very clear and they're like, "Oh yes, that makes so much sense. You have such a great talent with that."

I think that the universe then also supports that. For me, I didn't have any business classes or skills. I didn't know what I was doing. Those are the kinds of things that I thought out. As far as writing a business plan and what kinds of things to do to support my career and my own professional development.

But then there really is the joy. When you're working in your purpose it's such joy there and that for me is the runner's high and when you are in the flow. When I work with clients, the hours just go by and I always focus on the results for them and what their vision is. It's not what my vision is, I tell them, let's work towards your vision of this space and support them there. When you're working in your purpose or expecting your purpose, it really is very clear.

Christy – You just talked about courses and personal development. What are some of the books that you read, training you attended or mentors you had that assisted you with being on the path you're on now?

Shannon – This is my first foray into being an entrepreneur, so if any of the listeners are thinking of becoming an entrepreneur, I would really support you to look at small business development classes.

Where I was in California, there was the small business development center. There are mentor places like SCORE. Look for any type of support system for developing a new business in your area. There will be specific ones for women, mentors, or asking for capital, if you are looking to produce a product and you need startup funds. There are all kinds of really affordable education out there for you if you are looking to start your own business.

For me, I wasn't producing a product. I was looking for a service, so the other side of what I needed was education. There is a National Association For Professional Organizers and that was something that I started going to. Local meetings at the San Francisco chapter and then I started going to the annual conference.

Then I got certified as a professional organizer through that Association. When you get clear about what your purpose is, continue to research how you can fully express that, both in business and through learning more about your professional development in whatever career path you're going towards.

Christy – As people are working, is it the clean break that they should make or is this something they can do to work themselves slowly out of their jobs? What's your take on that?

Shannon – I think it really depends on the person and their profession, and certainly what their financial commitments are. That's a really very personalized response to that. I think for a lot of people, it's important to go at it slowly and test the waters and maybe do things at night or on the side.

It is so easy these days to put up a website and you can get a separate phone number. There are all kinds of ways you can easily start out slowly. Part of developing a business plan is doing the market research to find out who your competition is and what would be an acceptable rate of what you charge. Those kinds of things.

It's really important to do the due diligence research ahead of time and then really see what is your comfort level in that because anytime you're transitioning to your own business, a new career, or a different direction, it takes a lot of courage.

I support anyone who is really ready to focus on their purpose to get coaching or training around that and get really clear about what's the best way to support you with that transition.

Christy – I kind of set you up on that question because a lot of people think that they need to leave their jobs immediately, then start the small business or they don't move towards it. It is a slow process and it's not going to happen overnight, but doing so almost refreshes your life because you're working towards something.

People are afraid to step forward because they think they need to make the clean break and then it will never happen. You can use your evenings and weekends to create the life that you desire, so we're on the same page with that answer.

As you talked about courage, one of the things that Napoleon Hill said was, "Definiteness of decision requires courage. Sometimes very great courage." I have that on my bathroom mirror and when I read it this morning and I said, "It does."

Tell the readers about courage and decision and how that affects the way we move forward in our lives.

Shannon – I'll frame that in the context of being a professional organizer and going back to the definition of clutter as something you haven't made a decision about. It does take courage to make a decision and I would also say that making decisions is like a muscle that you just need to build up again.

It's a practice that you need to strengthen over and over again. With those decisions that you make, even if it's something basic like the papers on your desk, or the emails in your inbox or whatever, that have built up into an overwhelming pile or mess.

You will gain clarity by making those decisions and from that clarity comes the courage to take the next leap or step, or whatever it is for you…baby step. Whatever courage looks like. Courage can look like baby steps or it can look like a giant leap. Having that clarity really empowers your courage.

Christy – It's almost like walking in the dark. Decision illuminates the path in front of you. It gives you the courage to step. So if you're not organized…it really goes back to being organized and having clarity in your life. Also, having the ability to not have your mind distracted by things that are overwhelming you. Regardless of what they are.

Making a decision is the first step to getting on the path that you're supposed to be on and then Providence, the universe or God will show up on the next step, but people have to make the step.

Shannon – Yes. I do think that having the clarity and clearing the clutter is really going to help them. I don't think you can be clear about your purpose until you can feel more and more clear within because your purpose comes from within.

If you can clear that...it goes to what you said earlier, the universe that surrounds you as far as your home and your office environment is really a reflection of the inside.

If you can continue to clear those spaces externally, in your home or office, or clear the space within, then that clarity for the definition of your purpose is going to come through. As well as the courage to take the leap or the baby steps to move in that direction.

Christy – One of the things that you mentioned earlier was, you talked about being in the flow. Tell the readers what it's like to be in the flow and working in a business that you love.

Shannon – One of the things that comes to mind first, as I mentioned earlier, time goes by really really quickly. That's a sign for me that I'm in the flow or making great progress. The other thing that happens for me when I'm working with a client is what I call "divine download."

If the client is stuck on something, I ask them several questions and then I just get this idea that comes to my mind and I ask them, "What about this?"

If it's something they can't find or they're not sure, I ask them, "Well...what about it going here?"

Just having those divine downloads, which for no reason I would know what their answer is, but I'm holding a clear enough space where I can ask a very directed question for them. So I'm really having a direct download for them in their circumstances and I always feel like that's such a great sign of me holding an open space and allowing the information to come through so I can help them think outside the box. To help them think of different ways to approach whatever they're feeling stuck with.

That's the second thing. So the time passing and the divine downloads. The third thing I would say is, particularly if I'm doing a home or an office, I can just walk into a room and see how it could be better laid out for the client's vision, in whatever way they're feeling stuck or overwhelmed. It really is that I have this clear vision of how it could possibly work better for them in a way they haven't thought of.

Just making suggestions, not that we have to implement them at all, but just that I'm thinking of something completely different that they haven't thought of. Those are the three things for me when I'm working with a client that I know I'm really in flow and I'm holding a space for the client to be able to make decisions and they're in the flow as well.

Whenever I'm in the flow, then obviously, they're going to be in the flow too because I think that's how it works energetically.

Christy – Absolutely. Can you give the readers two pieces of advice that can get them on the path to organizing their life and organizing what they need to do to get clarity on their vision?

Shannon – Sure. One of the things that I always encourage people to start with is, to focus on what's working because everybody wants to talk about what's not working. They just want to focus on the problem areas, but I also think it's important to switch your perspective and focus on what's working.

Do they like their desk? Do they like their chair? Do they like their office space?

What's working in there that really supports them to be their best. Also, taking that list of what's working and then crafting it into what's the vision. What do they want to have to take that to the next level? What is the vision that can pull them towards their goals?

For some people, it could be changing the location of their office. It might be what else they could do to personalize it or sometimes it's over personalized, and it can be really over stimulating.

If they want a very simple, elegant or modern feel, what is that vision and how are they going to get there? If they want it to look more professional...whatever it is. In that case, I would say, start with what's working, because that will help you change your mindset and then say, "In an ideal world, how could I perfect this even further? Those two things are a great place to start, rather than focusing on the clutter or the overwhelm.

Christy – I love that. That's gooood. You talked about joy earlier and before I left my career, I hadn't felt joy in a long time and we only think about joy as a Christmas ornament. Share with the readers, what is joy to you and what does it feel like? Some people have lost that sense of what that really means, other than what we see at Christmas time.

Shannon – That's a great question. I think it really applies to all of our readers today who are really looking at their purpose and thinking about a really bold move and possibly changing careers. I think that joy is something that comes from within that isn't about external circumstances. I think about happiness as based on external circumstances. Like, I'm happy with that color or new pillow or whatever new thing I get.

Joy is really something that just bubbles up from within. Very much for me when I'm on purpose and being of service and helping people create transformation in their lives. That brings me a genuine joy, as well as the things that I do for myself that I enjoy. We can think about the word "enjoy" as well and that gives you a lot more options.

The things that we enjoy doing are the things that bring us to light and they can be very simple or basic like reading or walking outside in nature or cooking, or whatever that expression is. It's an expression of the joy you feel within. That is a direct correlation of being on purpose.

Christy – Shannon, thanks so much for assisting the readers with finding their purpose. It's closer than they think and is usually something they're naturally good at, which may not be in alignment with their careers. You're fantastic!

Chapter 7

My Greatest Shame Liberated My Soul
Debby Montgomery Johnson
Video – www.bit.ly/manifestdreams-Debby2

Debby Montgomery Johnson recently expanded her Purpose by releasing her book and starting her movement, *The Woman Behind The Smile.* In this interview, Debby is going to share the story that led to this movement. Debby, tell us a little more about yourself.

Debby – I started off years and years ago at an attorney's office. I was a paralegal there and got some legal training for a few years. But, instead of going to law school, I decided I wanted to go into the Air Force. I spent eight years as an Air Force officer in imagery intelligence. I loved that job. I learned a lot about the world and people. I really enjoyed working with the government and I learned there how to keep secrets. After I was in the Air Force, I spent 11 years at home with my family. I raised four children, several of whom are now military officers.

Then I decided when my husband was going overseas with the Air Force as a contractor that we needed some medical insurance and I decided to go back to work and chose the banking field. I became a manager for World Savings Bank and Wachovia Bank and that's where I got some financial background.

I did that for six years and then decided to get out of the high-stress environment of retail banking and went to be a school treasurer for the school district of Palm Beach county, Florida. I did that for a couple of years until I had a major change in my life when I got a phone call that my husband had passed away. That's when I completely changed what I was doing and the focus of my life.

Christy – We've had conversations about being the President of a company that your husband started and now shifting into what you want to work on, which is stepping into your purpose, in addition to keeping the company, keeping the customers happy and doing what needs to be done. Share with us more about how you shifted into The Woman Behind The Smile.

Debby – It was really difficult at first because I was thrown into running the company when Lou died and I knew just a little bit about it. Fortunately, I had the resources of customers and vendors that I had worked with, who were very kind to me and helped me keep the company going. I learned a lot of how to keep it going, with productions and that sort of thing.

I tried to do my very best to market and speak about the company, and I have a passion for the product, but I didn't know enough about it from the medical side and that held me back. I felt like I couldn't promote the company as best as I should because I couldn't go out there and talk to doctors, and that held me back.

I struggled for about a year on how I could make things better. I went to training, like Sharon Lechter's Dedicated Entrepreneur and I got up there and did my 90-second pitch and it was not something that came flowing out of my mouth. I did well, but it just wasn't my passion and I realized the company was Lou's passion.

He was a diabetic. He had neuropathy and he found something that alleviated or reduced the pain and he was very passionate about that because it helped him personally. As I struggled with realizing that it wasn't my passion, I asked, "What is my passion?"

A friend of mine said, "Deb, you've been living your life as a mom, an intel officer or whatever. Who are you and what do you want to do for you?"

The reason my passion is The Woman Behind The Smile is because after Lou died, I spent six months just working as hard as I could to keep the company going and I had no life. I was working two jobs at the time. I'd go to the elementary school in the morning and work there until mid-afternoon and I'd go swimming, which is the one thing I did for myself.

Then I'd come home and work on my company from 2 o'clock in the afternoon until 2 o'clock in the morning. I had no life and I didn't like to go to sleep at night because I was alone in my bed after 26 years of being married. It was sad for me, and I'd get up the next morning and go to work.

A friend of mine said, "Deb you need to get a life and you need to start dating."

I hated dating when I was 16 and I really didn't want to date again when I was 52, but I was like, "I'll try it" and that's how I got onto the online dating scene.

I kind of dipped my toe in and stalked for a little bit. I was just looking around to see what's out there. That led me to what I thought was a really terrific friendship/relationship. It lasted for two years, and it was an extraordinary international event, but I never met him in person. I talked to him. I emailed him every day. I journaled every single day. I kept all the emails and texts and whatever I got from him, and I had about 3000 pages of journals that chronicled our love affair…is what I'll call it, even though it wasn't an affair.

Christy – Wow!

Debby – Yeah, and so I thought he was going to meet my family. He had a little boy and a sister and he had been widowed also. He was from London and an international businessman, so we had a lot in common. I was able to basically use our relationship as two years of therapy because I wrote everything down about my life, about Lou dying, and about the kids. I just got all my feelings out, as I would talking to a therapist.

At the two year point, he got online one day, we had very spiritual discussions, he said, "How do you feel about forgiveness?"

We went on and on for hours about how I felt about forgiveness and I said, "Why are you asking me this?"

He said, "Because I have a confession."

I'm like, "What are you talking about?"

That's when he confessed to me that the whole thing had been a scam and that he needed my forgiveness because he needed to be able to move forward. I guess he had some type of spiritual awakening, and felt like the only way he could move forward is if he confessed to me and asked for my forgiveness.

It was awful! It was an extraordinary experience, but it ripped my gut out. It was worse than when Lou died, because at that point, I had been personally involved for two years. Financially, spiritually, emotionally, I invested my whole life into this man.

Literally…and when it got pulled out from under me, I was shaken to the boots, down to my core. I tried to go to the FBI and they said, "We're sorry, but we can't do a thing for you because he's out of the country and unless you get him here, there's nothing we can do. We can't recover any of your money, we can't recover anything, we're sorry. But, thanks for coming in and telling us your story, we'll put it in our database."

At that point, I shut down emotionally, because I felt so violated and financially it just destroyed me. I was ashamed of what I had done. Here I was an intelligent person. I had the finance background with banking. I had the intelligence background from the Air Force. I had the legal background from working with the law firm and I was completely duped because my heart ruled my head. At that point, I was afraid to say anything because I felt so stupid for being taken so badly.

The only people I told were my parents because I had gotten them involved at some point and they came over immediately. They went to the FBI with me and my dad said, "This has got to be a movie. This is an unbelievable story and it's unbelievable that you, who are so well trained, could have been taken so badly."

I hid that for years, even from my children. It wasn't until I went to speaker training with the Women's Prosperity Network down here in Florida, about October/November 2015. A woman and I were having lunch together and she was saying something about online dating and I guess I rolled my eyes, and she said, "What's that about?"

I told her my story and she said, "You have got to get that out."

I said, "No, no, no. I'm too scared. I can't possibly tell that story. I'd look like an idiot."

Over the weekend, they said you have got to tell that story and one thing led to another and I ended up telling my story and it was mesmerizing. It was empowering to me and I thought, this is my passion. I am so tired of men and women being taken by scammers and the problem is no one talks about it because they are ashamed of what they've done.

I declared, "I'm not going to be quiet anymore. It's my passion! It's my movement to get us to speak about it because it heals your insides to be able to do it."

It also makes you realize that it doesn't matter what other people are saying. It's your life! You made the choices, you suffered the consequences or live through the consequences, but what can you do for good to keep at least one more person from being hurt, or scammed in the future?

That's my goal now. My goal is to get it out there and get people to speak about what happened no matter how embarrassing it is because it doesn't matter what other people think. It matters what you think. It matters what you can do to move forward and not hold yourself back because of the shame.

Christy – You and I spent some time together in October 2015 at Sharon Lechter's Speak Serve and Sell event and I've seen how you've transformed in energy and spirit and how color is coming into your face. Your spirit is shining through now, not that it wasn't then, because you were good then, but there's something different about you.

You talked about speaking, but someone gave you permission to speak about what you're most passionate about, so I can see how your energy, your face, and everything has changed about you for the best. It illuminates who you are because you're now working in your passion. I just want to applaud you for that.

Debby – Well, thank you. It's just an amazing feeling. It's the energy. It's the stand up and I just want to stand up! When I talk to women at church or other organizations, I just get so energized and so passionate about women, in general, speaking up. Speaking up no matter what.

It's amazing to me how people come to me and say, "I was taken in a Ponzi scheme, not one, but two." Or, "My mother got scammed for $80,000 because she answered a phone call."

Darnit! As a banker, it really irks me, because they are so savvy. When I went to the FBI and they said they couldn't do anything about it, they explained to me it's an international web of deceit and it is so difficult. If you think of it like a spider web, it's so difficult to get to the beginning and by the time you try to shut one down, they've sprouted another and it's all around the world.

It's sad that people are so evil that they'd do this to such trusting people as I and others. It's just sad, but it's life. It's just life and you can't let it stop you.

Christy – This is interesting…a little side note. About two months ago, I got approached by someone on a freelance site and they said I had a job and I spent 20 hours with these people doing training. It was a very educated person, so it's not shocking.

They got me for my time, but they asked me for money. It was a couple of things that happened where my red flags went up and when they asked me for money, I was like, "Not gonna happen!"

But it was a very high-level scheme because they sent me a package overnight and I could track it with the postal service. It was an $18 package, so they spent a lot of money for this scam. It showed me that, one, there is a higher level of treachery out here in these streets and it was very intricate where they had me spending 20 hours with them.

We think about our backgrounds and who we are and there are scammers out here in these streets. I applaud you for saying it because I would never tell anyone they got me for 20 hours.

Debby – They start little. I think about the way mine started and it was a little innocuous thing, where he said, "I have this friend that wants to get onto the dating site and his credit card is not working, can you send him the money for it?"

It may have been like $10-$15. I said, "Sure I can help out."

Then he's like, well if she'll do that, then maybe what else will she do? Little by little. They weave the web of their life story into yours. It's so compelling and before you know it, you're sending them $50,000 or $100,000. It happens.

It's not just online dating, it's every day. Someone sends you a check and wants you to deposit it and give them the money back. That takes a toll on a lot of the elderly people down here in Florida. I used to see that at the bank all the time. Someone would come in to cash a check and they're supposed to send money back. A friend of mine's mom got scammed last week when someone called up and pretended to be her grandson and said, "Grandma, I'm in trouble. You have to send money right away!"

Instead of going to her daughter to find out the grandson was right there in the house, she sent money. Her instincts of "let me protect my family" kicked in and she did it.

As soon as they get your credit card, blip, you're done. They can get anybody at any time. What I found interesting from the FBI, was here in Palm Beach county, men get taken so much more, for more money than women, because they're looking for love too.

These guys get taken by a picture of a pretty girl and we want to help. We're kind people and we want to help and unfortunately, you get taken when you're in some situations and it's sad. It burst my bubble of trusting people and that was the hardest for me. I'm a very trusting person to this day, but like you said, when those red flags start waving around, I pull back.

That's the lesson I had to learn. I pull back, but I don't initially believe that people are bad. I want to talk to them. We are in the business of trust.

Christy – It's all starting to make sense now. Us spending time together, you're awesome, but then you became Super Duper Awesome'er.

Debby – That's a great word.

Christy – Yeah…it's completely not a word. Lol! But, you're so passionate now. Again, your whole being and face and your posture, everything has changed about you.

It's been nearly five months, tell us how it felt to be set free from when you finally admitted it on a large stage. How did that feel to you?

Debby – It was the most liberating, amazing feeling I think I've ever had in my life. Because I found a voice. I found *my voice*. I mean, I have given briefings and done things all my life. But because I was able to get that shameful thing I had done out in the open.

The FBI said, "Don't be ashamed, you did nothing wrong, you were the victim."

I don't want to be a victim. But it happened to me. I didn't want to have that label, and I'm not. I'm not a victim. If I had labeled myself as that I could have stayed that way and I didn't want to be that. I've never been that way. I've always been a go-getter and achiever. I'm a high achiever sometimes…in my quiet way, but I've always done well. This one I did really well, but it wasn't a good thing to do well at.

It's been a very encouraging time. When I talk, I stand up. I walk around. That's where my energy is, just flowing out with this thing. I didn't have that when I was talking about my company because it was Lou's company that I'm just running.

One time you'd asked me how I'm dealing with the opinions and judgments of others. For the most part, people have been very encouraging and very supportive of what I'm doing. That's how I could have done this in the beginning. The hardest part was letting my children know, my oldest boys. I caught it pretty hard and I totally understand why they felt the need to really blast me. It was done in love.

Christy – How old are they?

Debby – Twenty-nine and twenty-eight. They're both military pilots and real go-getters and bless their hearts. They had taken on the role of man in the house. Even though they didn't live here with me and at multiple points during the two-year affair, the boys would say, "Mom, don't ever send him money and don't get involved."

I heard all these don'ts, but I thought, "I'm an adult. I'm the grown up here. I can do what I want to do and I'm taking care of the family."

I think they felt that I had betrayed the trust I had with them and that I didn't listen to them and honestly, I didn't. That was my fault and I had to apologize from the bottom of my heart and I said, "Boys, there is a reason this happened and there is a reason it's happening to me because it's happening to a lot of people in this world who will never talk about it."

I had a woman tell me one time, "I think you were chosen to have this happen to you because God knew that you could do something with it and you could talk about it."

That's what I told my boys. This is my passion now. This is my movement to go out there and try to make a difference for just one person and if I can make a difference for hundreds or thousands or the world, great! But I just want to save one person from going through this heartache.

I have the resources to move forward. I have the friends and family and background to not get stuck. I can put my foot forward and take one more step and one more step and one more step. I'm going to make something of this because it's so important.

Bad guys just make me mad! There's my passion. I'm just mad. Well, not mad, but frustrated that it can happen to so many people so easily and no one knows about it because we don't talk about it. Twenty-five million people were defrauded last year and that's only half because the other half don't talk about it. No reports.

Christy – Dr. Myles Munroe said, "Every person was created to solve a problem in their generation."

We're too busy working in our jobs and not working in our Work which is what God put us here to do. So yes, you are that strong woman who "got duped," but it's also happening to other smart people and people who are not so smart. It's happening to the elderly and the young and the men. I can see how you're going to make a huge impact in the world. I'm excited!

Debby – We are given a purpose and we're here because we're articulate and smart, and we can get the message out with passion and love and we're not trying to take advantage of anybody.

We want to get out there and assist people in whatever troubles they're having. That's us. That's us as women. We've always been of service. When we were in the military, we were in service of our country. That's a part of us and I think that part of me really needs to come out.

I'm doing it in my company step by step. I have my dad helping out, which is great. He's the voice of the company and he has great compassion for people. But he sees how I've grown personally from this situation. From being totally devastated financially to moving forward and getting the word out.

It's exciting for the family and I have a different relationship with my kids now. They're like, "Mom before you do anything, just let us know what you're going to say."

But, I go for it. Just go for it and make a difference in the lives of people around you and make a difference in this whole situation. That's what I'm trying to do.

Christy – I can't wait to see how this unfolds for you in the next couple of years. One of the things I want to share with the readers. You had two choices. You talked about being a high achiever, so you're now able to use this to serve other people or you could become a victim.

What is your advice to the readers who've had devastating challenges in their lives? What's your advice for them to try to find the peace in that or find the glory in that situation to be able to serve other people?

Debby – Honestly, I came up with seven steps and they're called, "Stand Up In Your Power." There are a few things that we all need to do. If you've been duped like me, you have to go to the authorities. You have to seek out the FBI, the bank, the post office, whoever it is that might be in charge of what happened to you. You need to go there and let them know. You have to report it.

The next thing to do is talk to a trusted person. Talk to a friend, talk to a family member but be honest. Find a safe place so that you have a place to speak up. For me, it was my group of women friends at the Women's Prosperity Network, at the speaker's training.

They listened to me, and their hearts melted with mine and they held my hand. That's what I needed to be able to move from victim to victorious because it's important to speak about it and get it off your chest.

The other thing that I found that I needed to do and this was at the beginning, I needed to forgive. No matter how badly I was taken, when he came to me and said "I ask for your forgiveness," I didn't really do it for him, I did it for me, because I've seen family members that didn't forgive over the years and it hurt them. It didn't hurt the other person.

I knew spiritually for me to move on, I had to forgive him so I could forgive myself and that's the hardest part is to forgive yourself, because we beat ourselves up more than anybody else can beat us up. The shame and the hurt. We hold on to that and until we forgive ourselves and let that go, we're not going to be able to move on.

The next thing that I did, which was very liberating and therapeutic for me, I call it, "Make It Noteworthy." I wrote it down. I wrote down everything in my journal and it was so refreshing. I thought I was writing down family history as it was going and it ended up being proof of what had happened, but it was very therapeutic for me to write it down.

The other thing is to take care of yourself. Deal with it and take care of yourself. For me it's swimming. I love to get out. I go to a water aerobics class, and I'm the youngest there by 20 years. I want to be like my old lady friends when I get older, but in the meantime, it gives me energy, it gives me a better feeling about myself, physically and mentally and that's really it.

The last thing is, you have to be unstoppable. You have uncovered who you are. Do some service, uplift someone, get away from yourself, get away from your home. I work in my home, in my office and the only time I'm out and about and around people is when I'm swimming in the morning. It was very easy for me to get sucked into this world between me and him online because I was at my desk. I was on my computer.

You need to get out of that area. You need to get out with people and do something for somebody else so you don't get stuck in your own little pity party.

Have power, gain power. I grabbed a parachute. I actually went skydiving. I've walked on fire. I've eaten fire and I've done these things that I never ever would have done, but it's been very liberating and fun.

My youngest son and I walked on hot coals last week with a fire walk. Off my bucket list, so I don't have to do it again. It was the mental preparation…that step is going to be hot, but the second one, not so much because you're going faster. So just get past the first one. That's what I've learned with this whole thing. You can be in the fire, but if you walk faster, you can get out of it.

Just don't stay there, get out of it! Walk fast and have that power and at the end go, "Power! Power! Power!"

Realize that you got everything inside of you what you need to move forward and be really great and that's what we need to do. Stand up and be powerful women and powerful men, or whoever. Not by taking advantage of others, but by lifting others up and being that one for other people and that's what I'm trying to be.

I have this friend that has this philosophy called the, "One Philosophy." It's where you are the one for the person you're with and they are for you. Or, you might be the one for the person you're walking past and you're smiling at that day. That smile might have made their day.

That's who I want to be. I want to be the one for whoever this is going to affect and I hope that it will be shared. I hope it will be shared so we're not sitting alone, being a victim in our own minds and in our own bodies and not letting go and moving forward.

So Stand Up! Stand Up in your power no matter what!

Christy – As you're talking, I realize you've actually become happier and more powerful after something that could have been so devastating.

Debby – Absolutely! I have. The happy story, and the end story with this is that I've found a wonderful man, local. We dated for three years and we ended up getting married in October 2015, so I'm remarried now and it's amazing. It's just amazing and he's so supportive of me and what I'm doing and it's been amazing. It's just an amazing story.

Christy – This is an incredible story and I look forward to continuing to dig into your story and pull those lessons out for our readers as we continue on this journey of life. Thank you Debby!

My Greatest Shame Liberated My Soul

Chapter 8

Unbecome and Reveal Your Purposed Life
Holly Nunan
Video – www.bit.ly/manifestdreams-Holly2

Holly Nunan is a Powerful Parenting Coach and children's book author. She's going to share how she surrendered her plan for The Plan and the dramatic shift that it's taken in her life for the best. Holly, tell us a little more about yourself.

Holly - Outside of what you covered in terms of what I do in the business arena, first and foremost I'm a mom. I'm definitely open to admitting that I totally lost myself in becoming a mom. That is something that was the beginning of the journey to who I am today.

I guess I bought into all these expectations that society had of me when I became a mom and I got so wound up in my responsibilities that I lost sight and forgot that I had a purpose for being here outside of raising children.

I'm very passionate about being a mom and how I raise my children. I'm passionate about how the entire next generation gets raised. I look back on my life and I can only see the limitations that were put on me and I'm aware of them, and I don't want to put them on my children. I'm contributing to how the next generation gets raised and I want to break some of the limiting belief systems so that we're not only raising a *new* generation but raising a *different* generation.

If we raise them the way that we were raised, we're just producing a new generation of us. It's definitely about evolving.

Christy – One of the things you said that I want you to touch on more is when you lost yourself when you became a mom. Tell us a little bit more about that, because there are a lot of people who lose themselves in whatever role it is. Wife, mom, teacher, or whatever their jobs are. Tell us a little more about how you lost yourself and how you knew you lost yourself.

Holly – I knew I lost myself because of the profound depth of unhappiness and unfulfillment that I experienced and I just saw myself wanting to do things that I knew kind of breathed life into my spirit, but I wasn't letting myself do them.

I was so wound up in meeting these expectations and I think everybody is, whether, like you said, being a parent or whatever their job or their role is within an organization or company, or society in general. We just buy into these roles and these roles come with a set of rules or a sense of what I call restrictions and responsibilities.

We get so focused on performing the role that we actually forget that there is a plan a whole lot bigger than our plan. By buying into the role or the rules of whatever plan we're following or what society said we should do and the expectations that society said we should live up to.

In order to live up to the expectations of society, I believe, for me and I speak on behalf of at least half the moms out there, in particular, you just become so incongruent with yourself. You divide this gap between your real self and what I call your representative. The one who represents who you really are.

How did I know? The feeling. I just knew it wasn't supposed to feel like that. I think everybody knows. I think we avoid admitting that we know because as soon as we admit that we know, we then have to take responsibility. It's a lot easier to be the victim because the victim doesn't have responsibility.

Christy – You said so much in that. In, *A New Earth*, Eckhart Tolle said, "Unhappiness is an ego created mental disease that has reached epidemic proportions."

The key in what you said earlier links to another quote from him. He said, "The thought is, 'I am not enough,' and other unconscious thoughts follow. I need to play a role in order to get what I need to be full in myself. I need to **get more** so that I can **be more**."

Holly – Yes! Yes!

Christy – What are your thoughts on purpose. What's your definition of purpose? Purpose and living in our dreams and who we want to be is never talked about in schools in America. Is that also not talked about in Australia? I thought that we were the only ones. Lol!

Holly – We would be exactly the same. My definition of purpose or the purpose of anything is the original intent for which it was created. Anything…like the purpose of a chair. It was created with an intent for people to sit on.

You can use it for other purposes. You can use it as a stool. You can stand on it, but it's never going to be as good at being a stool as it will at being a chair because that was the purpose it was created for. That was the intent behind its creation.

When it comes to our purpose, it's the original intent for why we're here.

Christy – Absolutely. I agree. Tell us about your journey and you talked about being a mom. How did you get into network marketing? How did you become an entrepreneur? Did you work before that, basically, how did you get on the journey that you're on today?

Holly – I don't know how far you want me to go back, but I'll tell you a story like I tell from stage and it kind of encompasses the whole journey for me. I distinctly remember at 14 years old, I made a decision and so resolved, that I would never ever, like ever, ever have a boss. I would never work for somebody and I would never ever, ever have a job.

The reason I made that decision was because I remember this day, I was so sick. I had tonsillitis. I was the sickest that I had ever remembered feeling up to that point and the only thing that I wanted was for my mom to stay home with me that day. I begged her, "Can you please not go to work and can you just stay home with me?"

She told me that she needed to go and call her boss and ask if that would be okay and I will never forget the sound. I heard her down the hall. I heard her hang up the phone. I couldn't hear the conversation, I could hear mumble jumble, but I couldn't hear the words. I heard the phone hang up and I'll never forget.

Even now I can hear it in my mind, like the click-clocking of her high heels on the slate floor down the hallway. I remember she stood at the doorway. She didn't even step in on my carpet and I think it's because she just felt awful about what she had to deliver to me. She told me he told her that she wasn't allowed to have the day off, but she could come home at lunch time.

I just made a decision. Number one, I was really annoyed at my mom, because I'm like, "Why did you even ask? Why didn't you just tell him, 'I'm not coming in?'"

So I definitely didn't feel important. I felt devalued. I just remember thinking, you know what, if that's what bosses do, I'm never going to have one. It's funny that you attract whatever you set your intentions to. All through school, I refused to even apply for jobs. My mom would put in resumes for me and I wouldn't show up to the interviews and things like that.

We used to argue all the time, but then I went to college, and I wasn't so sure, so I started looking for businesses. I worked casual for a place, not for the purpose of having a job, but for the purpose of having my foot in the door because I was interested in that industry.

Long story short, I got an option there before I finished my degree, to become a franchisee. Then we became a franchisee and two years later, we performed really well in our franchise. The franchise at the time wanted to expand, so he approached us to come on board as shareholders and help expand the company and that basically put me in the wellness business and here's the thing, I made this decision.

Here's what I decided. I made the decision that I would never ever take advice from anyone who doesn't already have what I wanted to have. In any area of life. Even in parenting.

I don't really care what kind of child psychology degree you have and how many books you've swallowed and can recite. Until your emotions are wrapped up in your theories and you actually have to parent a child that you love and care for, I can't take advice from you on how I should parent my child.

On the same token, if you didn't have the lifestyle that I wanted, the finances and the freedom, then I just couldn't take advice from you. Maybe at a very deep principle level, to the point where no intentions of disrespect, but it didn't matter what label you came with. Whether you came with the label of being my mother, brother, best friend, or my auntie, whoever you are.

The label doesn't make a difference to the principles. If you don't already have what I want to have, and I don't mean any offense, but I cannot afford to use your thinking to make my decision because your best ability to learn how to think, your best ability to make decisions your whole life has landed you at your life and your age. If that's not what I want, then I can't use your thoughts to make my decision.

I was aware of that when I was 18, coming out of college, looking for jobs and things, still anchored to that emotion I had at 14 that I'm just not open to that. That was it. So, I went okay, where do I find these people? It was a subconscious question without even knowing the laws of the universe at the time that I put out there. I just made it a point to find the people who already had the things that I wanted to have.

This is a big thing for me. I don't just mean in the way of materialism with cars and houses, but the people that give the way I want to give. The people that impact the way I want to make a difference. People that I could look at and say, you know what, I actually want to be you.

Those people and I just went out front and said, "Hey, I've made a decision that I don't want this life, but I don't know how to get the life I do want. Would you be open to a conversation?"

That's really where the entrepreneur started for me. Just, oh my gosh, being blown away by their level of thought and then allowing myself to take that on as my own thinking.

Christy – You just talked about not taking advice from people who don't have the results you want because that applies across the board, for everything. I've read a lot of studies on leadership and how women should lead. There are women giving advice on what women leaders shouldn't act like in the workplace. I think to myself, "You've never managed a lot of men because your advice is not sound."

You read that somewhere and you've never had a lot of men work for you and you're telling me how I should act and how I should govern myself at my job on how I deal with men based on what you've read? You don't know what you're talking about!

Same thing with you. If you have someone trying to tell you how to parent your kids and their kids are running amuck. People can't tell you how to make money and they're broke. I applies all across the board.

Holly – Exactly! So, that's my journey. One mentor led to another, who led to another. Along the way, I evolved. I wouldn't say that I became who I am, I would say that I unbecame who I had been taught to be and underneath all of that in the process of unbecoming, I found who I am.

Christy – One thing that I really like about you is that you turned that situation with your mom into your purpose instead of falling down and becoming traumatized. I've seen people who've had experiences in their life that they didn't necessarily appreciate and they're still talking about it and using it as a reason for why they're not who they want to be or where they want to be in life.

You didn't use it as a crutch. You were like, "You know what, I'm never going to work for anybody!"

Holly – Exactly. I used the pain as my fuel.

Christy – I love that. You said you attract what you set your intentions to. Share with the readers your insight on intentions and attracting. What is your definition of that and how has that come to fruition? Expand on setting intentions and how powerful that is with the laws of the universe.

Holly – Here's what I know. I used to say, here's what I think. It's not here's what I think, it's here's what I know. I've experienced it. I've lived it. The universe responds to results. It sends you what you ask for once you've asked for it. In that process, essentially it comes down to you making a decision. I say, "To decide is to eliminate alternatives."

I think that's the difference between wanting something and expecting something. People say I want these things, but until you have eliminated any other alternative, there is no resolve in what you want. The universe can only respond to your resolve.

It's like going to McDonalds and saying, "Can I have a burger?"

They'll say, "Sure you can have a burger, but we can't fill your order and actually bring it to you until we know what burger you want. What do you want on the burger?"

You can't tell the universe, "Give me success."

It needs specificity in the order to fulfill it. For me, it comes down to resolve decisions. What I mean by that is, there is no other alternative. Anything else isn't an option. I'm not someone who believes in Plan B because I think that when you have Plan B, basically you're telling the universe you're already planning for Plan A to fail.

For me personally, I'd just rather know I have resilience and that I can handle anything and I just work on Plan A. If it just so happens that Plan A doesn't work, at that point then, I'll take my message from the universe and will redirect myself, but I don't need to plan the redirection now because all that's telling the universe is that I'm not resolved in Plan A.

So, more often than not, Plan A doesn't happen because you got a backup.

Christy – How did you use that when you launched your children's book? Share with the readers about the resistance from other people when you set this goal, but what you did anyway.

Holly – Right. I guess the journey leading up to that, my revelation was, up until I started finding myself and even knowing there is a purpose in life and that I had one, everything I was focusing on was always, "What am I going to do with my life?"

Through this process, it changed to, "Who did I come here to be?"

Once that becomes your focus, like, who am I and who am I here to be? Not what I'm supposed to do? What you're supposed to do is already assigned to the person you came here to be. You actually don't even have to work out what you need to do. It's the default.

You already have an appointment. You just got to work out who it is you are. Who you came here to be congruently and authentically, at the core of your spirit and once you know who that is, you don't need to work out what you need to do. It's already organized. The instructions are already there. The appointments are already there and you just kind of roll with it.

Once I realized that and I started putting my focus on who I am, not what I do, there's this whole unveiling process that happened. I realized, very quickly, that there is a very big difference between *my plan* and **The Plan**.

There's a plan that's a whole lot bigger than mine and I kind of realized there are some decisions I don't get to make. When I get my own universe I can make up my own rules, but while I'm in this one, I've got some rules I've got to play by and I can never deviate from those rules. That was my first thing.

I was in network marketing and doing well. I was the number one leader in Australia, and I started hearing *the voice,* if you want to call it that. I just started getting pulled towards the gift I knew I had. I've always grew up writing poetry and I was getting passionate about what people were doing with their kids and what I was doing with my kids.

I was going to readings with my children and I was so annoyed at the books these kids were reading. I'm like, "You're spending all these hours downloading all this software on to your little hardware, your brain, and I can't believe your parents let you read this. This is just rubbish!"

That really was the beginning of the whole parenting journey where I'm at now. It started with the moment of being pissed off really. Then I definitely had to listen and it was hard. I felt like I was going to lose my identity in order to take *this path*, that I knew was not *my path*.

These were not my plans. I was trying to tell the universe, "I hear you. I'll get to you in a minute, let me just get to my thing first. Once I get my thing done. Once I get the promotion I'm going for in my company, then I'll pay attention to you."

What I realized was there was another plan and the more I tried to force my plan, it just didn't happen. I believe we have something, I call it the internal guidance system. It's like this GPS system on the inside of you and if you'll just be quiet enough to pay attention to it, you actually know what to do. You'll know whether you're on target or off target. Like a GPS system says, "Do a U-turn. Do a U-turn. Do a U-turn. You're going the wrong way." That started getting pretty loud.

For me, it was giving up resistance and being able to have faith and trust in something that I couldn't put on a spreadsheet and I couldn't quantify and I couldn't draw out on a plan. Like I literally had to follow it with nothing other than faith and in all of that, these feelings came back.

These vibrations…these emotions that would bring me to tears for what I would see as no reason. I believe that was the Divine God.

I went, "Okay, it looks like my plan is being interfered with by this other thing, so maybe I should pay attention to that and see what happens."

Like I said, your appointments are organized. I feel like I haven't even tried. I feel like all I've done is given up *my* plan and trusted in *the* plan and I definitely haven't tried like I did when I was working on my plan.

People ask, "How do you do it?"

I don't even know. I just listen. I pay attention. I just became obedient. I stopped trying to manipulate the plan.

Christy – Two things I want to touch on. You're living out the destiny of people who've had massive success by living in their plan. You said, "To decide is to eliminate alternatives."

Napoleon Hill said something like, "Burn all your bridges behind you and cut off all sources of retreat and that's the only way you're going to keep the mindset and have that burning desire to be better."

You mentioned there was a big difference in *your plan* and *The plan*. TD Jakes and Dr. Myles Munroe said, "If you want to make God laugh, tell him your plan."

Dr. Munroe also said, "God doesn't care anything about your plan." Lol!

Keshelle talked about sitting and getting into a quiet space and then asking, "Who am I and why am I here?"

You said, "Who am I here to be?"

She talked about getting quiet and listening. She also said what you hear will startle you because it's not going to be what you thought it would be.

Tell the readers how you got to the point of giving up your plan because giving up your plan is not easy, especially for strong willed women.

Holly – Definitely. I thought I was going to let a lot of people down when I did that. It wasn't even just about me. I was using all these things to convince myself why I shouldn't do it. I'm going to hurt these people. These mentors that have invested so much of themselves into me and I don't want to disappoint them.

I recently made the decision to leave the network marketing industry so that I can give my full attention and my full focus to what I know I'm being called to do. It was so painful. It really was so painful, but it's supposed to be. There's purpose in that pain because pain is the point from which we expand and if we don't expand, we actually can't get on target with our purpose.

There are people who still play that victim game or still use the things that happened in their lives as the reason for why they don't do something. Then they say they're looking for their purpose. There are lessons in all of that.

As soon as you can see the lesson in the pain, you get extension and as soon as you become this new evolved…new level of yourself, from that level of extension, it's like the voice is able to reach you.

But it can't reach you at that other level. You've got to participate in your own rescue. You can't just say I want this to happen. You've got to create the environment yourself and involve yourself in things that will help you learn those lessons and it is painful. But you have to allow the pain, trusting that you have the purpose, even if you can't see it.

For me, listening to that voice and giving up that resistance and that process of oh my gosh, this has been my identity for so long and how am I going to let go of that?

Here's the thing. You can have fear or faith. They can't coexist. Just like darkness and light can't exist at the same time, nor can fear and faith. When there's darkness, you don't sit there trying to work at how do I get rid of the darkness? You just turn the light on. You bring in the light, you don't remove darkness.

I relate that to fear and faith. This is a bit scary. I'm a bit concerned about what's going to happen here, there or whatever. What people are going to think? But, that's a focus on fear.

I changed my focus to how do I beat fear? How do I stand up and be this tough person that can just stand in the face of fear? If there is a presence of fear right now, I know that can only be true if there is an absence of faith. So, my problem isn't the presence of fear, my problem is the absence of faith.

When all of the sudden you shift into the faith of what you're going to…the price of what you're going to pay to leave stuff behind doesn't even come into your realm of thinking anymore. I just had to allow it to be what it was going to be. I didn't even put thought to it.

The old me would have needed to work that out, but the new me went, "Okay, I don't need to worry about that. There are plans bigger than mine and that plan will take care of that."

Christy – Earlier you talked about some of the feelings that you got whenever you stepped into who you were supposed to be and the hair stood up on my arms. When you're giving up your identity of who you think you are and when you get over letting people down, the feeling you get when you give it all up, I call it "grace."

It's that feeling that you've never felt before and you say, "Oh my God, this feels so good." So, it makes the pain and the insanity of going through the pain worth it.

Holly – Absolutely! Yes! Yes! It's a feeling that you know you've never felt before. You know you've never experienced it before. It's just new. It feels light and the old me would have interpreted it as scary, but here's what I think, we interpret it as scary, but it actually isn't scary. That's just the words we use to describe it. We just misinterpret it as scary.

What I believe is that's how you know that God, the higher intelligence, the Divine or whatever it is that people call that energy, that's how you know it's with you. Because what you want to do, it's supposed to scare you.

If it's your purpose, you're not supposed to be able to do it without the intervention of that source because you're just the messenger. It has to be too big for you to do on your own. You can't actually see how it's going to play out. If you could see how it's going to play out then you can play that role on your own and that doesn't have anything bigger than you behind it.

That feeling that was always interpreted as fear, I started to see that as comfort. I started to see that's the presence of the thing that created this whole thing. That's how I kind of say it to myself. I'm not scared right now, that's how I know I'm being guided. I'm being used right now. Something else is using my body right now type thing.

I just started to put a different mindset around that feeling, so I wasn't scared of it. I thrived on it. Now I love it. I connect to it all the time and sometimes I sit there in that feeling when I want something or I do something and later on, I'm like, "Dude, did I just write that? I did not write that. It did not come from me. Something else used me."

Like you said, in the beginning when I was all wound up in my plan, I was always ambitious, driven, a go-getter and all those things, but now I'm able to still be ambitious, still be driven, still want to win, but I can do it with a sense of grace in me. I'm not in control. I don't try and control it now.

Christy – No…because you can't.

Holly – That feeling that you say…feeling grace is a perfect word. That feeling is the feeling of grace and I think some people interpret it as oh my gosh it feels scary or nervous, but it's just their interpretation.

Christy – What are two actions that readers can take right now that will get them on the path to their purpose?

Holly – The first thing is this and this is my biggest principle that I teach and the biggest thing that I feel like I've lived. I believe that success in any area of your life, it doesn't matter if it's relationship, parenting, work, career, whatever, is more about learning what not to do, than learning about what to do.

Most people don't get what they want, not because they don't want it bad enough or don't want it as bad as the next person. They're not willing to give something up in order to have what they want. The universe can't give you what you want, it can only give you what you've got space for.

My belief is if you have more than three priorities, you don't have any. If you have more than three, you don't have any. So, work out what those three priorities are and once you know what those three priorities are, you then make a decision to eliminate alternatives. There is no other option. I just don't do anything that's not aligned with those three priorities.

I don't even have to go through the decision making process. It's like my decision is already made in advance. I don't have to spend energy or thought space making decisions every day because they're made on my behalf based on my decision to focus on my three priorities and anything outside of those priorities just doesn't get done…and I'm okay with that.

What that has shown me is, one thing I had to give up was not wanting to be in a popularity contest. I used to like being popular and liked being recognized to the point where I needed it and that was one thing that I had to give up. Doing all these things where I would get pats on the back and recognition.

The first thing is to figure out what your three priorities are and start working out what not to do. Not *what to do*, but *what not to do*. What are the things you can stop doing that as soon as you stop doing them, there's space for something else to come in and for you hear that voice or whatever that is? Work out what not to do.

My second thing is…I was actually trying to find the book that I referenced this from…I cannot remember the author, but I never forgot the lesson that I got. The book was talking about your purpose and here's what you work at, you work at what you love.

What you love is a clue to the assignment you were sent here to complete. What you hate is a clue to what you've been assigned to correct. I call it "focused fury." Where you can transform what you can't tolerate.

What can't you tolerate? What do you hate? What grieves you is what you've been assigned to heal.

I always teach people to work at what you love because somewhere in there your gifts are already there for you to complete that. What do you hate and get yourself what I call focused fury and what grieves you? What really hurts your feelings? What makes you go, "That is just not okay with me? It's actually so not okay, I need to do something about it."

Because from that place, you're not playing a popularity contest. When you're in that place, you don't care what anyone thinks. Who you might offend. All of those inhibitions are broken off of you and you just find what your message is and once you find your message, you find your millions.

Those are three things for me. Learning what not to do. Working out my three priorities and getting very clear on what I love, what I hate and what grieves me. With all of that, pay attention and allow yourself to be redirected.

I was stuck in a company and I was telling myself it's not working. I need to make it work. I need to make it work. The reason it wasn't working and I wasn't getting the promotion I wanted is because that was how the universe redirected me.

That's how it gets your attention. If it worked, I wouldn't have paid attention to the plan. I would have stayed right on my path. There was a reason and a Plan B making it not work. I had to stop seeing that as what am I doing wrong and go ok, "What am I being redirected to? Something is trying to get my attention and that's how I'll work it out."

Christy – It's almost one of those things where the universe stops you from doing something that's so easy and you say, "I don't understand why this isn't working."

So, you have two choices. You can continue to push and push and push and get frustrated. But this is when you're wanting to answer the call right?

Holly – Yes.

Christy – When you get silent enough and then you're asking the question, and nothing is working, that's when you see it. Because if you're not answering the call, you'll just go on with it and succeed and not be happy or get that feeling that you're looking for.

Holly – Exactly and then you'll see the difference. This is one of my favorite things that my mentor taught me, Mr. Jarrod Wilkins. I remember this resonating so deeply with my spirit. When he said, "The fruit is never for the tree. You never see the apple tree eat the apple. Your gift is not for you. It's for the benefit of people who will feed from your tree."

So, you have an obligation to work at what your fruit is and then I believe you have a responsibility to use that gift to serve the masses, because if you don't…it's not even about you. It's not even you that misses out.

You don't miss out if you don't share your fruit. You'll still get your nourishment from other people's fruit. It's other people that can nourish themselves from your fruit that miss out. When I started to really see it like that and I'm starting to get what you're saying about redirection.

I can hear that calling and a part of me wanted to resist it. I said to myself, "Holly this is not fair. You're being so unfair. You reckon you want to impact people's lives. You reckon you want to be significant. You reckon you want to change the world, all these things and right now you have a gift that comes so easy to you that can nourish other people so much and you aren't willing to leave that hanging from your limb for them to access. That's really unfair and selfish."

Christy – Woooo weeee!! Holly, you said a lot there!! Always a pleasure to get insight from you and I appreciate you sharing your wisdom with the readers. I'm sure they've been touched immensely by your words.

Chapter 9

Write The Vision, Make It Plain
Keshelle Davis

Video – www.bit.ly/manifestdreams-Keshelle2

Keshelle Davis is an educator, author, trainer, and trailblazer. Keshelle is a Master Dreamer and Law of Attraction enthusiast and uses the Law of Attraction to get what she wants.

Keshelle, tell us more about yourself.

Keshelle – I'm simply an entrepreneur by heart. I'm an educator. My passions include starting and creating new businesses and teaching people. That's really what I've been doing for the last 16 years. Teaching people the necessary skills and giving them the necessary information that allows them to grow their business, careers, and life.

Prior to that, I worked in banking, so I understand what it means to count people's money and after three years of that I realized I like to count my own money. That's really what brought me into entrepreneurship and I've been in the training and development industry for the last 16 years or so.

Christy – A lot of people don't know what purpose means. We're not taught that in school or anywhere and somehow people just come across that term and try to figure out what it is. What's your definition of purpose?

Keshelle – Purpose is a word that a lot of people hear often, but may not quite understand what it means. I have to go to the definition of Dr. Myles Munroe and he spoke a lot about purpose and in the simplest form, it's when you know and understand what you were born to accomplish.

I believe that everyone knows that they were placed on earth for a particular reason. That's been said quite a few times, quite a few ways, but very few people know and understand what that reason is. Purpose is when you know and understand what you were born to accomplish.

Of course, your goal is when you understand that, you continually pursue that and fulfill your assignment.

Christy – You mentioned Dr. Myles Munroe, who I love. Dr. Myles Munroe was an incredible and powerful leader who impacted millions of people all over the world. You're one of his students and disciples.

Tell us what it was like working with someone who talked about vision and purpose and Kingdom Principles before he was called home to be with God in 2014. What was that like working with such a powerful, powerful spiritual leader?

Keshelle – That's a loaded question because even to this day, I can still feel the impact of working with him, being surrounded by him and learning directly from him in such a strong way. I guess the way I can describe it is when you left his presence, no matter how long or short it was, he left you with something that you had to chew on for quite a long time because it was such a profound statement or a revelation.

I always left him wondering, "Where does he get this from?"

I would say that almost every week when he was home, he traveled a lot, I would always wonder where he got deep powerful truths from. So, he always left you with some nugget, no matter what the topic was. Some nugget that really forced you to stop and think, evaluate your thought process and he really changed your mindset.

Speaking for me, he changed my mindset in so many ways, on so many topics. He was really someone that the world lost, that made a tremendous impact in many many many people's lives.

Christy – I didn't know who Dr. Myles Munroe was until after the accident, and wanted to give you an opportunity to share who he was because he made an impact on you directly by working with him.

After his accident, I asked, "Who is this person that people keep talking about? Who is this person that the world is mourning? Who is this spiritual leader?"

I could see what his impact was based on the leaders who started talking about him. I did some research and saw some of his videos on YouTube. He was so profound, I bought a notebook to take notes from him and I watched 20-30 videos...at least. He was so powerful in the things he talked about.

A couple of weeks ago, I got an audio he did about 14 years ago, *The Power of Purpose, The Power of Vision*, from Audible.com and I've listened to that audio 12-15 times. It's about an hour and a half and it's soooo powerful.

Some of the things he talks about with purpose and vision is amazing, I recommend the readers check it out. It's $2.

He said, "Most people get a career and not a call. So our jobs become a prison because we never find out what our work is. Your purpose is your work. Your job is what they pay you to do."

Based on our work and our jobs, what's your take on what he offered in that statement?

Keshelle – Before I comment, I've read just about all of his books and one of my favorites is, *The Purpose and Power of Vision*. That's really what has inspired me to continue to host the Dreamboard parties and really share the work he's done through that particular book.

Unfortunately, we have been brainwashed to pursue a job. From primary school to high school to college, we are trained and guided towards finding a job. Whenever I share my story, I talk about leaving my "good government job," because people thought I was crazy when I left the bank, first of all. When I left my good government job, people thought I had gone insane.

Most people feel comfortable and secure when they have a job, but recognize that 90 percent...and this is just my opinion as I've taught hundreds and hundreds of people in my career and business. Only 10 percent realize or have that ability to connect their purpose to their job. Most people are on their jobs because it makes them money, but they are so unfulfilled.

They feel like failures because they know they are not doing what they were called to do or born to do. They feel frustrated and one of my favorite quotes from Dr. Myles is, "The poorest person in the world is the person without a dream, but the most frustrated person in the world is a person with a dream, that doesn't become a reality."

A lot of people have dreams. I've been doing my Dreamboard parties for the past five years. There are many dreamers out there, but a lot of them haven't made those steps to make it a reality, particularly because they are so caught up in the day to day efforts of their job to make a living. But they are failing to make a life of what they were called to do.

Christy – That's powerful! There's a survey from Gallup that says, 87 percent of people in the world, 2 out of 3, go to jobs every day that they don't like. Purpose is our work. It's what we're here to do.

One thing that Dr. Myles Munroe talked about was, every person on this earth was created to solve a problem in our generation. That is our work, but we go to jobs. That's not our purpose, that's our lifestyle. Sometimes we get caught up in these material things and we think they're going to make us happy when actually working in purpose and doing what you love and serving the world is what makes you happy.

Keshelle – Most definitely, but it's people like you and me who understand that and we should share more and more of the word. It saddens me sometimes to understand just how many people are on drugs that they really don't like and unfortunately, some don't have the strength to make that change.

Christy – Why do you feel that people stop dreaming?

Keshelle – Because of the process that it takes to bring that dream to reality. A lot of people have dreams and visions. They believe, especially those who aren't taking any steps to making that dream a reality. They believe it's easy. They believe I see what I want and I'm going to be able to accomplish it pretty quickly, but it doesn't work like that.

One of the *12 Keys To Making A Dream Real* is process and the process towards fulfilling that dream and vision can be rough, tedious and extremely difficult to say the least. There are stories upon stories of people who went through any number of things to make a dream a reality.

Christy – Rough is an understatement. Lol!

Keshelle – Yes, rough is an understatement. Lol! That's a lack of a better word. I think that a lot of people fall short of the process. A lot of people give up in the process. A lot of people get tired and frustrated in the process.

After a while, there are some who say, "You know what, it's more comfortable to quit."

You know that whole comfort zone thing. It's more comfortable to stop and stay where I'm at. Unfortunately, a lot of people are like that. It's the process that make or break those people.

Christy – Steven Furtick, a fantastic pastor that's in Charlotte said something like, "The middle is when you determine whether you have a fantasy or a vision."

The middle is the testing ground for what you're going to do and what you're going to work on because if high levels of success and living in your dreams was easy…and I don't want to discourage our readers because it's awesome, but it's not easy. If it was easy, everybody would have it.

People look at Oprah, Mark Zuckerberg, Elon Musk and the founders of LinkedIn and Twitter and they think that they're going to get rich quick. Or they think that these people had three months and they became very wealthy. Not knowing that it was a five and six-year process. Six years to have your dreams tested to see whether or not you're going to last and fulfill your purpose and your mission and not have that fantasy.

Keshelle – When you were speaking, it reminded me of a quote that I wrote in my book, *Your Child Can Become Wealthy*, and it says, "Everything looks like a failure in the middle."

Halfway through baking a cake, in the middle, the kitchen is a mess. Most people, if you're not clear and you're not strong enough and not wise enough, we look at the middle and say, "Okay I'm a failure. I feel like a failure, I look like a failure. I must be a failure and I give up."

But those who strive to the end recognize that there is a beautiful cake at the end of this process, that they are eager and willing to do what's necessary to make that a reality.

Christy – Absolutely! Let's back up two steps because we got in the middle without getting at the start. We scared everyone and I hope people are still reading. Let's talk about the beginning. How did you make the shift from banking to your government job to now living in your dream? What was it like for you? Did you make a clean break and jump into the darkness or was it a process where you worked yourself out of your job? How did it play out for you?

Keshelle – That's a funny question. I'm a risk taker, so I pretty much jumped off the cliff. I was always entrepreneurial and I was always a dreamer for as long as I can remember. In my teens, I always said I wanted to live the life I dreamed about. Never knew what that was quite clearly, but I just had the desire. My dream was to always be free and live the entrepreneurial life.

In 2008 after I started, I think it was my third company by then, I started a company Creative Wealth that teaches financial literacy principles to youth, young adults, and families. It was then that I recognized, this is something that I was extremely passionate about and it was extremely new to the market here in the Bahamas.

I just was a risk taker. For me when I recognized that it was something that I wanted to do, I left my good government job. I gave them my two weeks' notice. Being a single mother at the time, people thought I was ridiculously crazy. I started my Creative Wealth company.

I will tell you it's been a roller coaster. I don't regret any moment of it, but I felt so strong about my call, my purpose, what I was born to do. I felt that was something I wanted to do and was connected with my purpose, so I went whole heartedly in. I jumped right in.

Christy – It depends on your level of risk and what people feel comfortable with. To live in purpose, to risk it all…you will risk it all and you have to have courage. You have to be able to withstand some of the comments from other people.

Share with the readers how you managed yourself among people who thought you were nuts for living your life the way you wanted to live.

Keshelle – It had to start from the top. My parents are traditionalists, so they really were the ones that said, "Keshelle, what are you doing?"

But for me, I made a point to surround myself with people who believed in me. So while there were those who wondered, "What is Keshelle doing? What will she do?"

There were those who would say to me, "Keshelle I have you back. Keshelle I believe in you. Keshelle go for it. Keshelle you can do it."

I believed in myself as well. It was that combination of faith, belief in myself and a very very strong support of people. It was a small group, but they were strong and mighty, who I found that regardless of what happens with the direction I was going in, I had some people I could rely on.

With those three things, faith, belief in myself and the strong support, I managed to grow Creative Wealth into a recognizable brand. I've started several other companies, initiatives, and brands since then and I love what I've been able to do.

Christy – I love the statement when you said, "Regardless of what happens." At the end of our lives, we don't know when, we don't know how, but in the last moments, what will we say to ourselves, "I wish I would have or I'm glad I did."

You won't know what will happen until you step out, but regardless, just know that it's going to be okay.

Keshelle – Yes! When I speak to people, I always ask them, what's the worst that can happen? Seriously, what's the worst that can happen? I've had some stories. The first book I wrote about some of the things that I went through, but I'm still here. I'm still alive.

I love being associated with people who are also called crazy people because the people that are called crazy are the multi-millionaires and billionaires today. So, I love it when you call me crazy. I'm an entrepreneur, so I talk to a lot of people who want to fulfill their entrepreneurial dreams and I say what's the worst that can happen. At the end of the day, you will have at least tried and known what your potential could have been.

I always believe that if you are a true entrepreneur or you're going after something that you're passionate about or you feel it's connected to your purpose, doors are going to open and one thing is going to always lead to the next.

Christy – What are two actions that readers can take right now that will start them on the path of figuring out what their purpose is and what they're called to do in this world?

Keshelle – Sit still. Sit still. Sometimes it's not always easy because we have a million things going on in our lives. For me, I've been known to just get away and I've done this many times. Get away and find a place that you feel inspired by. For me, it's the water, the beach, it's nature.

Find a place where you can be very quiet with your thoughts. Then ask the source, God or whoever your source is, "Who am I?"

Sometimes you may not get the answer right away, but keep asking that question, "Who am I?"

Sometimes you may be startled by the response, but that's the start, in my opinion, in identifying who you are. Also, ask, "Why am I here?"

As you consistently begin to ask those two questions… I remember the first time I asked that question, I didn't get a response right away. That's not a question that you just generally ask out of the blue, but I kept asking. I kept searching. I kept seeking and eventually I began to get the answers.

Fast forward 7-8 years, in 2015, I did it again as I was looking to uplevel my life and move to the next level. I did the same process. I sat on the beach one Sunday morning and I spent hours there and I said, "Who am I? Who am I now? What am I going to do?"

The answers are there if we are truly open to listening. I think some of us are afraid of who we truly are and what we are truly born to accomplish. When I do these dream board parties, I hear things like that.

One Friday night, I was hosting a dream board party and a girl said that she is so afraid of what God has shown her and who she's seen herself to be. She's afraid of that and doubted what she's seen because it's so big. She doesn't see herself ever being able to live up to that.

I think that's where a lot of people are. In some inkling or some shape or form, they know who they are, what they were born for and called to be, but they are not accepting it for whatever reason. Most reasons are fair and because of that, we don't allow ourselves to pursue it.

Ask yourself who am I and what am I here for and begin to seek and search and listen for the answers.

Christy – Before we move to the second point when you said you asked, "Who am I?" I actually got chills because I remember asking that question about two years ago. I was already an entrepreneur and working in purpose. I wanted to get more clarity around what were the expectations and I was also startled by what I was shown and I said, "That is preposterous!" Lol!

"That right there is not going to happen! I can't even imagine how I'll get to be THAT person."

I was overwhelmed with the answer and one of the things that Dr. Myles Munroe and TD Jakes talks about is if you could do it on your own, then it's not big enough.

Keshelle – Yes!

Christy - If you can accomplish who you're supposed to be and if you can accomplish the vision that you just asked for by yourself and without the creator, God or the universe…if you could accomplish it by yourself, then that's not what it is. It's so big and it's overwhelming.

As I was on the phone with my coach earlier today, and I realized that I have become THAT person. This is who I am. How I show up in the world. How I respond to adversity. How I respond to other people and their negativity or other people and their positivity.

TODAY I am the person that can carry out what I was shown two years ago.

Keshelle – It's having that belief again. You should do it afraid. If you're reading this, you should do it afraid. The things that I've seen in my future, I wonder the same way, but the difference between success and failure, purpose and just living an unfulfilled life is recognizing, you know what, that's what I see. I have no clue how that's going to happen.

I say that to people all the time. Don't worry about the how. Focus on what you see. Focus on the dream. Focus on the what. Make the step. Even if the step is a tiny step, a tip toe towards the vision that you see, continue to make those steps, because you'll be amazed when you look back and you connect the dots, how it all evolved.

Christy –You talked about sitting still and asking. What's the second thing readers can do, and the actions they can take to get them on the path?

Keshelle – I have to talk about the dream board. Write the vision, make it clear, regardless of what it is that they see. They have to get clear to the point where they can basically see what their life will look like. Their future vision and I do my dream board parties for that simple reason.

Prior to hosting my dream board parties, I taught financial literacy principles and wealth creation principles and it was so funny that everyone wants to create wealth. Everybody want to be financially free and have a lot of money, but money is a tool to reach your dream.

So, if you don't have the dreams, it's very difficult to create the why, the passions or the motives towards going after or pursuing wealth creation. Getting very clear by writing it down and putting the pictures where you can actually see them and that will inspire you each and every day.

Even those days, we all have those, when you're down and feel overwhelmed or tired. When those days come, you have something that will remind you of why you were born, what your purpose is and what that dream is you're looking at.

You haven't asked this, but I'll go on. If I could give a third thing, I would say give yourself permission to dream.

Christy – YES!!!

Keshelle – It saddens me how so many people, whether society sees them as successful or not, I've worked with some of the top corporate professionals, CEOs, and it saddens me that many of them do not give themselves permission to dream. They live a life and go through the motions based on society's standards, that they should be here by that time or there by this time.

During my dream board parties, there's an activity I do where I challenge them to look at the end of their life. Look at the day they would die and ask, what are their regrets?

The regret is they've not allowed themselves to dream. They haven't given themselves permission for whatever reason. Give yourself permission to dream.

Christy – Wonderful! Keshelle, I value you and you are a Law of Attraction expert...and you're brilliant. I appreciate you not only offering your value to the readers in what you know and what you've learned as you offer your story, but I also value your friendship. I appreciate you supporting this project and supporting the global vision of making this world a better place and keeping the dream of Dr. Myles Munroe alive.

Write The Vision, Make It Plain

About The Authors

Christy Rutherford

Christy Rutherford is the President of LIVE-UP Leadership, a leadership development and training company. Christy is also a certified Executive Leadership Coach and assists companies with creating cultures of high performance.

Christy Rutherford served over 16 years as an active duty Coast Guard officer and is the 13th African American woman to achieve the rank of O-5 in the Coast Guard's 245+ year history. Her tours expanded from: drug interdictions on the high seas; emergency response/dispatch to hundreds of major/minor maritime accidents; enforcing federal laws on 100's of oil/hazardous material companies; responding to the needs of the citizens in New Orleans two days after Hurricane Katrina; a Congressional Fellowship with the House of Representatives and lastly a position that benefited from her wide range of experience.

A Harvard Business School graduate in the Program for Leadership Development, Christy also earned a Bachelor of Science in Agricultural Business from South Carolina State University, a Master of Business Administration from Averett University, a Diploma Sous Chef de Patisserie from Alain and

Marie Lenotre Culinary Institute, and a Certification in Executive Leadership Coaching from Georgetown University.

Among her many professional accomplishments, her national recognition includes the Coast Guard Dorothy Stratton Leadership Award, Cambridge Who's Who Amongst Executives and Professionals, Career Communications STEM Technology All-Star and the Edward R. Williams Award for Excellence In Diversity.

A speaker and best-selling author, Christy recently released four books, which can be found on Amazon and Kindle. Shackled To Success, Heal Your Brokenness, Philosophies of Iconic Leaders *and* Philosophies of Spiritual Leaders.

Christy offers three free resources:
1. Free E-course – Take Inventory, Get Flaky People Out of Your Life! www.christyrutherford.com/takeinventory
2. Work-Life Balance Assessment -
www.christyrutherford.com/worklife
3. Free Quote cutouts – www.christyrutherford.com/quotes

Connect with her on social media:
LinkedIn: www.linkedin.com/in/christyrutherford
Facebook: http://www.facebook.com/christyrppc
Email: liveupleadership@gmail.com

Debra Banks

Owner and Lead Business Consultant at TNC (The Numbers Count) Business Consulting, Debra has spent 30+ years of using numbers to run corporate departments, grow her own businesses, and to generate millions in sales for her teams and others. She brings skills and experience from both her formal education and her lessons from the school of hard knocks.

Debra earned a Bachelor's in Finance and MBA from the University of Virginia. Her extensive career and experience includes positions at large and small companies in positions of finance, marketing, accounting, and operations.

An entrepreneur, Debra built a successful business for over two years and ten sold it. She's also built a team of direct sales people that are still delivering results today. Debra has been an owner or partner in several other businesses and gained more experience (and armor) from those business building efforts.

She supports businesses in improving operations and increasing profits by making the numbers count for their business success. She assists clients with increasing their sales and profits and through her methods and coaching, she guided an event promotion from losing $40,000 annually to being profitable.

An author and speaker, Debra teaches her audiences how to embrace the numbers to make their businesses thrive. Her favorite motto is "Show me the money!" To that Debra says, "If you want me to show you the money, then you need to show me the numbers."

Debra is a yoga instructor. And she also enjoys jazz music and playing with her grandson, Sammy.

Get Debra's free resource, "The Numbers Tell The Story" at http://www.peakprofitsmethod.com/

Keshelle Davis

Listed in The Nassau Guardian's "Top 40 under 40" for the 40th anniversary celebrations of The Bahamas Independence, Keshelle is well known for her ability to educate empower and inspire others. She is currently the Executive Director of the Chamber Institute – the education arm of the Bahamas Chamber of Commerce and Employers' Confederation (BCCEC). Keshelle has also founded and leads The Training Authority, an independent training company where she established herself as an expert in the area of corporate training, program design and development and support for new and established trainers. She is also Founder and President of Creative Wealth Bahamas, a non-profit organization that provides financial literacy and wealth creation education for youth, young adults, women and families.

She is a columnist for the Nassau Guardian and has been featured on many radio and television shows within the country.

In 2006, Mrs. Davis became the Founding President of FFL Investments Ltd. (The Future Female Leaders Investment Group). She heads a team of empowered and driven ladies who have started the journey toward financial freedom through business, investing and education. She is also a mentor and inspiration to many up and coming female entrepreneurs through

Girlfriends & Co – an organization she founded dedicated to supporting women entrepreneurs.

Keshelle has competency in various professional backgrounds and industries—banking, IT, security and investigations, government, business administration, training, sales, public relations, marketing and human resources.

She is the recipient of many international professional certifications including: Certified Technical Trainer (CTT+), Certified Business Professional Executive (CBPE), Certified Administrative Professional (CPS/CAP), Microsoft Office Master Instructor and Application Specialist. She has been recognized as a leading female trailblazer by the Iron Network organization and has won awards namely Executive of the Year, Speaker of the Year, Rising Star and others.

Keshelle is a former member of the Rotary Club East Nassau and a past President of Toastmasters Club 3956. She is a founding member of the Organization of Young Professionals (OYP), and has served on several other boards such as the Surrogate Aunt Program of the Willamae Pratt Center for Girls, International Association of Administration Professionals (IAAP), Sunny Isles Chapter; the Bahamas Society of Training and Development (BSTD). She sits as Director on the board of the Bahamas Chamber of Commerce & Employers' Confederation (BCCEC) – the youngest female to ever serve in such capacity

Keshelle's passions are training, reading, meeting people, travelling, and horseback riding and pursuing new business opportunities. Keshelle is the author of the book, "Your Child Can Become Wealthy" forwarded by Sharon Lecter (co-author of Rich Dad Poor Dad and Think & Grow Rich for Woman) which was released in 2010 and has been featured locally and internationally.

She is married to Dr. Glenn Davis and the mother of a beautiful daughter, D'shelle.

Keshelle offers a free 30-minute consultation. Go to www.meetwithKeshelle.com

Dr. Emily Letran

Dr. Emily Letran is a general dentist who owns two multi-specialty group practices in Southern California. She received her Bachelor of Science in Biology from UC Riverside (magna cum laude, Phi Beta Kappa). She is a graduate of UCLA School of Dentistry (Dean's Apollonian Scholarship) and received her Master of Science in Oral Biology from UCLA at the same time.

As a mother of three, Dr. Letran creatively balances work, family life, after-school life and her personal life as a growing entrepreneur. She continuously takes courses in clinical dentistry, practice management and marketing, attending multiple business forums every year, striving to improve her skills to better serve patients.

Her favorite activities include reading, writing, and "hanging out" with her three children - whether playing tennis, watching Netflix or window-shopping at the mall.

Dr. Letran is an author of several books:
From Refugee to Renaissance Woman, On the Inside Press
From Zero to Hero in Ninety Days, On the Inside Press
Out Front – Business Building Strategies from Frontline Entrepreneur, Celebrity Press
The Ultimate Guide to Having A Beautiful Smile That Transforms Your Life, Perfect Publishing

Commit: Embracing the Big Life, Celebrating the Entrepreneur's Family, Business, Passion, and Fun Perfect Publishing

Contact Emily at www.exceptionalleverage.com

Shannon McGinnis

Shannon McGinnis is Founder and CEO of Organized 4 Success. She is a Certified Professional Organizer, sought after speaker, and author of two instructional organizing books: *The 10-Minute Tidy: 108 Ways to Organize Your Home Quickly* and *The 10-Minute Tidy: 108 Ways to Organize Your Office Quickly*.

Shannon works with executives and entrepreneurs who are overwhelmed by the paper and digital clutter in their offices to transform their chaos into systems that save them time and money. She and her team of consultants provide on-site or online confidential, non-judgmental organizing assistance for residential and corporate clients world-wide.

Contact Shannon at shannon@organized4success.com

Get Shannon's free resource "12 Tips To Eliminate Excessive Email Forever" at – www.organized4success.com/

Debby Montgomery Johnson

Debby Montgomery Johnson is a woman on a mission. In her book, "The Woman Behind the Smile" she shares her personal experience with a love that turned into betrayal and financial disaster and she removes the mask of shame and shows others how do to the same. Many of us have something, something we're hiding, something we're ashamed of, something that through no fault of our own or through our own making, something that we keep hidden and that, in turn, keeps us hidden, from each other and the world.

From Vermont and a graduate of Phillips Exeter Academy and the University of North Carolina-Chapel Hill, Debby is the President of Benfotiamine.Net, Inc, a vitamin supplement company that provides an alternative for the pain of neuropathy, a nerve disorder. (Benfotiamine.Net). Benfotiamine makes an extraordinary difference especially for diabetics and their families.

Her background is diverse, from working as a paralegal and bank branch manager to being a U.S. Air Force officer, serving as an Intelligence Officer at the Pentagon, the Defense Intelligence Agency and in Wiesbaden, Germany. Debby is just like you. A woman on a mission to live an authentic, joyful life as the Woman *WITH* the Smile rather than behind it.

Contact Debby at Debby@TheWomanBehindTheSmile.Com

Download Debby's free resource, "7 Steps To Stand In Your Power" at www.thewomanbehindthesmile.com/

Get her book, The Woman Behind The Smile at – www.bit.ly/womanbehindsmile

Holly Nunan

Holly Nunan is a wife, mother of 3 girls, an entrepreneur, a powerful business woman, a leader, a parenting expert, an international best-selling author, and a highly sought after motivational speaker and trainer. Her ability to teach an audience, and deliver a message that resonates with their soul is unparalleled. Her work doesn't just "inspire and motivate", it leaves a lasting impact on the lives of those who are fortunate enough to cross her path.

She made a decision at 14 years old that she would never have a boss. Ever. She did not believe in the way society had programmed us to live, and she had no intention of playing any part in such a limiting system.

At 19, she started in business, buying a franchise in the Health and Fitness Industry. By the age of 22, she became a part owner, and franchisor of that company. Over the next 8 years, they grew the company to 65 franchises across Australia, and were named inside the top 30 fastest growing franchise groups inside BRW's Fast Franchises list, 4 years consecutively. At the age of 31, they sold this company, and retired from traditional business.

At the age of 26, Holly was introduced to the industry of Network Marketing. With a 2 year old and a 4 month old at the time, and a husband that travelled too often, Holly knew that if she wanted things in her life to change, SHE had to change some things in her life. It was this industry that introduced her to the world of personal development, where Holly began to discover her true self.

After becoming the number 1 income earner and producer within her company throughout Australia, Holly made her announcement to leave the industry in December 2015 to answer the call that was on her life, and give it her full attention.

Holly loves to help people build their minds, through a process she calls "Unbecoming". She assists people in identifying and releasing old and limiting belief systems, and birthing new ones that serve a greater purpose in each person's life. She is bold, she is honest, and she is laser focused with her vision.

In September 2015, after much demand, Holly launched a website based around "powerful parenting" and "pursuing your purpose", which had over 5000 views within 24 hours. Through this website she is teaching parents all around the world how to raise TODAY'S children for TOMORROW'S world. She teaches parents how to break free of the programing of society, that leaves us to be so limited in our thinking, so unfulfilled in our hearts, and so off target with our life's purpose.

Holly teaches parents how to empower their children to live congruent, authentic, empowered lives, which leads them to discover their own life's purpose.

In November 2015, Holly wrote her first children's poetry book called "What is an idea?" Hundreds of hard copies were sold within days, and when the book was launched on Amazon, it became an International number 1 best seller in every category within 24 hours, surpassing Dr. Seuss! In January she released her second book, titled "Broken crayons still colour" and expects to have her series of 10 completed this year.

Holly is in the process of completing an entire series of books, each which is written in poetry, and each with a message that will touch the spirit of every child, deepening their sense of self-belief, self-esteem, self-worth, and self-love. In addition, she will also be releasing her parenting books in 2016 also.

You can connect with Holly, and join thousands of others in her Facebook groups where she builds communities of people with similar beliefs, and provides immense value for those on their spiritual expansion journey.

To become part of her ever-growing communities, go to

Powerful Parenting
www.facebook.com/groups/PowerfulParenting

Unbecome – Spiritual Expansion
www.facebook.com/groups/200965433594938/

EXPECT Success, and Stay Amazing!!

Made in the USA
Middletown, DE
30 May 2020